MORE JOY IN HEAVEN!

Kevin Doran

MORE JOY IN HEAVEN!

Confession, the Sacrament of Reconciliation

THE LITURGICAL PRESS
Collegeville, Minnesota

Cover design by Scott Kerr.

Nihil obstat: Richard Sherry, D.D. *Censor deputatis. Imprimatur:* ✠ Joseph Carroll, D.D., Dublin Diocesan Administrator.

The author and publishers are grateful to the following for permission to use their copyright material:
Hamish Hamilton Ltd and Alfred A. Knopf for Albert Camus, *The Plague;* Faber & Faber Ltd and Harcourt Brace Jovanovitch Inc. for TS Eliot, *Murder in the Cathedral;* AD Peters Agency and Alfred A. Knopf for *The Stories of Frank O'Connor;* Gujarat Sahitya Prakash for Anthony de Mello, *The Song of the Bird;* Deborah Rogers Ltd for Kasuo Ishiguro, *An Artist of the Floating World.* Extracts taken from *The Jerusalem Bible,* published and copyright 1966, 1967 and 1968 by Darton Longman and Todd Ltd and Doubleday & Co., Inc., are used by permission of the publishers; excerpt from the English translation of *The Roman Missal* © 1973, International Committee on English in the Liturgy, Inc. (ICEL). All rights reserved.

First published by Veritas Publications, 7-8 Lower Abbey Street, Dublin 1, Ireland. This edition has been authorized by Veritas Publications for sale in the United States of America and Canada only and not for export therefrom.

Printed in the United States of America.

1	2	3	4	5	6	7	8	9

Library of Congress Cataloging-in-Publication Data
Doran, Kevin.
    More joy in heaven! : confession, the sacrament of reconciliation
/ Kevin Doran.
        p.   cm.
    ISBN 0-8146-1824-3
    1. Confession—Catholic Church.   2. Reconciliation—Religious
aspects—Catholic Church.   3. Catholic Church—Doctrines.
I. Title.
BX2265.2.D655   1989   89-15343
234'.166—dc20   CIP

What man among you with a hundred sheep, losing one, would not leave the ninety-nine in the wilderness and go after the missing one until he found it. And when he found it, would he not joyfully take it on his shoulders and then, when he got home, call together his friends and neighbours? 'Rejoice with me', he would say, 'I have found my sheep that was lost'. In the same way I tell you, there will be more rejoicing in heaven over one repentant sinner than over ninety-nine virtuous men who have no need of repentance.

(Luke 15:4-7)

CONTENTS

FOREWORD

One particular moment in St Luke's gospel puzzled me for years. It occurs in chapter five when Simon Peter finds himself faced with a miraculous catch of fish — after having had a night of total failure. Why at that moment, when amazed by the overflowing nets, does he fall at the knees of Jesus and say 'Depart from me Lord, I am a sinful man'? Why think of sin at that point? Would it not be more natural to give thanks?

I had an insight into this through hearing the experience of another Peter — a student in University College where I teach and where Kevin Doran is chaplain. This Peter was planning a twenty-first birthday celebration for himself. Being far from his family, he decided to invite a large circle of his friends to gather in a pub on the particular evening. At first many of them accepted but as the date drew near, most of them made apologies for being unable to come along. Eventually Peter was left with only three or four companions for the outing. He tried to hide his disappointment but within himself he was feeling let down. At one stage the few friends suggested to him that they would enjoy themselves better in a quieter place — so why not go back to his flat? Without much enthusiasm he agreed. But when he opened the door of his flat and put on the lights, he had the surprise of his life: the place was all decorated and everyone he had invited was there — and more — all singing 'happy birthday'. Peter told me that he sat down on a seat near the door, amazed, delighted, but overcome with a sense of unworthiness. He felt unworthy of so much care.

Simon Peter must have moved through that pattern too — from a sense of failure through dawning gratitude to a sense of sorrow and of sin. Perhaps it is only when I am in touch with the love of God that it is safe to face my unworthiness. Unless I first know myself surrounded by the fullness of his gifts, my sins could lead to self-concerned guilt rather than to liberating sorrow. It seems to me that at the heart of the problems that people find with the Sacrament of Reconciliation is that it is seldom *experienced* as a prayerful moment of healing.

Kevin Doran's book aims to open the understanding of the reader to the life-giving aspects of this sacrament. He writes with common sense and honesty, but most of all with pastoral concern that people would not miss the blessings of this encounter with the forgiveness of Christ. Drawing on his own experience, he has put together a book that should help many to think out again their approach to this most human of the sacraments.

Several years ago the Irish Catholic Bishops wrote a pastoral on *Handing on the Faith* and raised the question as to how many people genuinely grow into adulthood in their religion: 'Are we going through our adult lives with ideas about religion more suitable for primary schoolboys and schoolgirls?' That question applies in a special way to the Sacrament of Reconciliation. The externalist approach learned as a child — and suitable for the psychology of a child — can linger long into life, so much so that 'going to confession' may never discover any mature way of expressing itself. Where people get stuck in what St Paul called 'childish ways', Kevin Doran's pages will surely spur them to get unstuck and to appreciate anew the rich potentials of this sacrament.

Michael Paul Gallagher, SJ
Department of English
University College, Dublin

JUST FOR STARTERS

Shortly after I was ordained but before I received my first appointment in the diocese, a friend of mine who was working in a parish in the city asked me if I would help him out by hearing some Confessions on a Saturday morning. It was one of the things I had spent seven years preparing for, and I looked forward to the opportunity of putting some of the preparation into practice. But, at the same time, I was more than a little apprehensive and felt very young and inexperienced as I made my way out to the confessional. The first few people who came for Confession didn't put me under too much pressure, and I began to feel a little more at ease. It wasn't destined to last; I drew back the screen to find a young man who said, 'Bless me father, I have sinned. I haven't been to Confession for about ten years, and I'm a bit nervous'. I was a bit taken aback, but I thought it was only fair to warn him, so I told him that it was my first day and I was a bit nervous too. He seemed to relax a bit. Maybe he felt we were in the same boat but, more than that, I like to think that maybe he realised that the peace and forgiveness he was looking for is a gift from Jesus Christ, who is able to offer his gifts even through young, inexperienced and imperfect priests.

Confession, or the Sacrament of Reconciliation, as it is sometimes called, is a situation where two people come into contact in a very personal way; a situation which calls for great honesty and trust. I believe it is also a situation in which God is working very powerfully to bring about renewal, healing and a change of heart. God's love can overcome the limitations of both the penitent *and* the priest.

The aim of this book is to look at some of the questions people

11

have about Confession, including the basic question about why there is such a Sacrament at all. I hope that it will also help to reassure those for whom the Sacrament of Reconciliation is a cause of anxiety.

I have drawn on my own experience, both as a priest and as a person who comes to Confession for forgiveness. One thing which is central to the Sacrament of Penance is confidentiality (the 'confessional seal'), so wherever I have given examples in the pages that follow, they have been 'created' from my general experience of the Sacrament, and do not relate to any particular person or any particular Confession. Throughout the book I have used the term 'penitent' meaning the person who comes to Confession. The use of the 'he' and 'she', 'his' and 'hers' etc. is not meant to imply any more than the obvious truth that some penitents are women and others are men, and in the vast majority of cases one could be substituted for the other without changing the meaning or the truth of the points being made or illustrated in the book.

In the early stages of the preparation of this book, I asked a number of people to read through it, and I am very grateful for the many helpful comments and suggestions which they made.

1

THE GIFT, THE FALL AND THE CALL

The gift

What kind of place is a hospital? Most people will tell you it's a place where people go when they are sick, especially if they are too sick to be looked after at home. Hospitals are bad news. For the people who work in a hospital, there is a slight but important shift of emphasis; a hospital is a place where people come to be restored to health, so that they can return to their families and their work and carry on with the business of living. In much the same sense our first thoughts about Confession are often to do with sin, whereas Confession, or the Sacrament of Penance, is really about being restored to God's friendship; about being reconciled. The story of Confession doesn't begin with sin; it goes back beyond it to God's love which has been given to each of us from the very beginning, and which has never been taken back. Speaking to his disciples Jesus asked:

> What man among you with a hundred sheep, losing one, would not leave the ninety-nine in the wilderness and go after the missing one till he found it? And when he found it, would he not joyfully take it on his shoulders and then when he got home, call together his friends and neighbours? 'Rejoice with me', he would say, 'I have found my sheep that was lost.' In the same way, I tell you, there will be more rejoicing in heaven over one repentant sinner than over ninety-nine virtuous men who have no need of repentance. (*Luke 15:4-7*)

What is the meaning of such rejoicing in heaven? It can only mean that God, for reasons which are beyond our understanding, values each person as an individual and never takes away his love. This love is the whole meaning of God's creation. We are made in his likeness, not in the sense that we look like him, but in the sense that we can come to know him, to share his life and

13

know his love. His first gift to us is his own love. The many other gifts of his creation are given to us, not to use just as we like, but to sustain us and to help us to become more fully what God has called us to be.

In this book I will look at the meaning of sin and forgiveness; I will look at how judgements are made about how Christians ought to live and I will examine the Sacrament of Reconciliation, how best to approach it and how it is celebrated. But, throughout, the one thing which gives meaning to everything else must be kept in mind; God loves me and will never take back his love. The Fourth Eucharistic Prayer celebrates that faithful love of God in these words:

> Father we acknowledge your greatness:
> all your actions show your wisdom and love.
> You formed man in your own likeness
> and set him over the whole world
> to serve you his creator,
> and to rule over all creatures.
> Even when he disobeyed you and lost your friendship
> you did not abandon him to the power of death,
> but helped all men to seek and find you.
> Again and again you offered a covenant to man,
> and through the prophets taught him to hope for salvation.
> Father, you so loved the world
> that, in the fullness of time, you sent your only Son
> to be our Saviour.

Against such a background, *More Joy in Heaven!*, while dealing with the reality of sin, is really about forgiveness and reconciliation, with a sense of hope and confidence in God's love which makes all things new.

The fall and the call

A few months ago, I was driving an elderly aunt to visit some other relatives. As we drove along, I remarked on the beautiful view ahead of us. The early evening sun was slanting across the hills of Dublin as it broke its way through here and there between the rain clouds. My attention was momentarily distracted from the business of driving and, too late, I noticed that the car in front had stopped at the traffic lights. The bang was terrible and, with a sinking feeling in the pit of my stomach, I got out to have a look at the damage. There was no way that either car could be driven away.

It's funny in a way but, even in a situation like that, there's a tendency to straighten yourself up and look around to see if anybody else has noticed. No matter how you feel inside, you try to act as if nothing unusual had happened, in the hope that you can hold onto whatever dignity you have left. The fear that things might be even worse than they actually seemed made me reluctant to examine the damage too closely. It was easier for the time being to hope for the best than to cope with the idea of repair bills and increased insurance premiums. I had always felt that I was a fairly good driver. Most drivers feel the same, I think. But there was no escaping the fact that this accident had put just as big a dent in my pride as it had in my car.

The pattern is often the same when it comes to damaged re-lationships. If I seriously disappoint a friend because I fail to keep a promise which I know meant a lot to her, the damage is done and there is no point in pretending otherwise. When I come in after a 'hard day at the office' and fly off the handle because somebody put onions in the soup, I end up making everyone else miserable because I had a rough day. But pride often makes it difficult to take responsibility for the damage. Sometimes it seems easier to put on a wounded look and to stand on one's dignity, hoping that not too many people have noticed.

Few people would claim to be perfect, and most of us are aware at times of needing to be forgiven. On the ordinary human level, there are times when we know that we have hurt or betrayed someone, and that only that person's willingness to forgive can restore the relationship. In a certain sense, the more she loves me and the more willing she is to forgive, the deeper will be the awareness of my failure to love and my need to be forgiven.

Restoring a strained relationship with God is not really very different. The first step is to recognise that damage has been done, and to accept responsibility for it. It helps a lot if I can accept that God is *always* willing to begin again. The idea that sin is something that I do which hurts God is not really very helpful, because it makes us think of sin only in terms of a God whose dignity is offended. It is nearer to the truth to think of sin in terms of the damage to a relationship which results from sinful attitudes and ways of acting. In this way it is easier to see that we stand to lose a lot more through sin than God does.

It's a pity that when we learn the Ten Commandments, we usually learn them in isolation from their context, instead of learning them as part of the Scripture passage to which they belong. The Bible doesn't just have God suddenly calling Moses and handing him the two tablets of stone. Long before this he has called Moses to lead the people out of captivity in Egypt. He has fed them and watched over them in the desert and has seen to their every need. He has invited them to find fulfilment in their relationship with him. At Mount Sinai the people are invited to enter into a solemn relationship, or covenant, with God, as their response to everything that he has already done for them. The terms of the covenant are that he will be their God and they will be his people. The Commandments which form part of the Covenant are seen by the people as God's gift to them, and the special mark that they are his people. His laws are not understood as restrictive, but as helping them to become truly free:

> You yourselves have seen what I did with the Egyptians, how I carried you on eagle's wings and brought you to myself. From this you know that now, if you obey my voice and hold fast to my covenant, you of all the nations shall be my very own, for all the earth is mine. I will count you a kingdom of priests, a consecrated nation. So Moses went and summoned the elders of the people, putting before them all that Yahweh had bidden him. Then all the people answered as one, 'All that Yahweh has said we will do'.
> *(Exodus 19:4-8)*

Many of the Psalms, the folk hymns of the Israelites, praise the wisdom of God's law, which 'gives life to the soul. . . wisdom for the simple. . . joy for the heart. . . and light for the eyes' (*Psalm 19*).

When we look on God's law as something given to his people for their own benefit, and as the way for them to reach happiness and fulfilment as his people, then it becomes possible to see that sin affects not just God but also the sinner himself. The sinner offends against himself because he rejects the way that leads to life. Take Paul for example; his whole pre-occupation in life is making money. He works every hour that God sends, pulls strokes whenever he can and suspects everyone who works for him of being 'on the make'. There is no doubt that profit has replaced God as the focus of his life. It is quite likely too that his strokes and his suspicion cause him to offend against justice towards other people, and his pre-occupation with his money-making leaves him little time for family responsibilities. It's easy enough to see how Paul's lifestyle offends God and those around him. But what kind of person has he become in himself? Is it not reasonable to say that he also sins against himself because he accepts a lifestyle full of anxiety and tension, in which he cannot really be fulfilled in his relationships, either with God or with anyone else?

Or take Brenda who is called to give evidence in a court case involving a charge of drunken driving and leaving the scene of an accident — a hit-and-run. She knows that the man who is charged is innocent, but she lies against him in the hope that by doing so she can protect her brother who is the real culprit. It's a difficult position to be in. We can easily see how her perjury is an offence against the innocent man, and against God who, on oath, is called as witness to a lie. But her perjury is also an offence against herself, because it makes a liar of her, and a lie can never lead to fulfilment with God who is always true.

Without the sense of God, our appreciation of right and wrong is very narrow; we love those who are close to us and expect them to love us in return. We only respect those who earn our respect. But God's love makes the world into a 'global village'. The fact that he loves me, means that I am called in response to love all those he loves. Fulfilment means being at one with God and with his friends.

The best, and certainly the best known, description of sin is the allegory of the fall of Adam and Eve in the book of Genesis. Immediately I hear people saying, 'Surely he doesn't expect us to believe that in this day and age?' Perhaps this is a good time to say that the Bible is made up of many different styles of writing. They are not all historical. Some passages are poetry and others are law, and still more are in the form of story. What the Church asks us to believe is not that everything in the Bible is *literally* true, but that it is true in what it teaches. So what does the story of Creation and of the Fall of Adam and Eve set out to teach us? In simple terms these first chapters of the Book of Genesis express the belief that everything that exists came about (directly or otherwise) as a result of the creative word of God. Before the Creation there was nothing. Everything God created is good.

'God saw all that He had made and indeed it was very good' (*Genesis 1:31*).

Finally, we are told that evil came into the world by the free choice of the first people who thought they knew better than God what was good for them:

> The serpent was the most subtle of all the wild beasts that Yahweh God had made. It asked the woman, 'Did God really say you were not to eat from any of the trees in the garden?' The woman answered 'we may eat the fruit of the trees in the garden. But of the fruit of the tree in the middle of the garden God said you must not eat it, nor touch it, under pain of death.' Then the serpent said to the woman, 'No! you will not die! God knows in fact that on the day you eat it your eyes will be opened and you will be like gods, knowing good and evil'. The woman saw that the tree was good to eat and pleasing to the eye, and that it was desirable for the knowledge it could give. So she took some of the fruit and ate it. She gave some also to her husband who was with her, and he ate it. Then the eyes of both of them were opened and they realised that they were naked. So they sewed fig leaves together to make themselves loin-cloths. (*Genesis 3:1-7*)

What counts here is not really what the first people were called or how many of them there were, or whether they lived in a garden. What is important is the truth of the message which is contained in the Bible text. Put very simply, the story begins with the happiness enjoyed by the people because of all the things God has given them, most of all his own friendship. The one thing they cannot have is to be gods themselves, to be the ones who have all knowledge. But they think they know better — they can decide for themselves what is good and what is evil. (Notice that in the story there is no mention anywhere of an apple, but only of the fruit of the tree of knowledge of good and evil). They realise, too late, that, sophisticated and all as they are, they cannot take the place of God. They sense their nakedness, their lack of any defence in his presence. They have betrayed his friendship. Their first reaction is for each to blame the other 'It was the woman; she gave it to me'. 'It was the serpent; he tempted me'. Passing the buck is a typical human trait. In the end, having set out to improve on their position, they finish by losing even what they had. Their selfishness is their own downfall.

It doesn't take too much imagination to transfer the scenario of Genesis to the world of our own experience. Dissatisfaction with what we have, selfishness, lust for power and the determination to 'go it alone', lead us to put ourselves in God's place and to think that we know best what is good for us. We scramble over each other in the effort to get to the top of the pile. Happiness is replaced by tension, fear and suspicion. When things start to go wrong, we blame each other. Will we too end up by losing what we started with — our friendship with God — by trying to be what we can never be — God himself? This is what sin is all about and it is found in the workplace and in the family, in children at play, in enclosed monasteries and in international relations, and wherever there are people.

Sin is not just what one person does against another. It includes the way groups of people harm or offend other groups of people through their political and economic decisions and actions. On a local level it might include the attitudes of the settled community towards the travelling community. On a more global level, the unjust structures which contribute to the huge gap in living standards between the developed world and the developing world, are no less sinful than the enslavement of one individual by another. Sin also extends to the way we harm each other and deprive future generations through our abuse of the environment.

Few people are totally evil, but few are really perfect either. The reality of sin points to the need for a change of heart, a turning back to the wise ways of God, a need for forgiveness and the renewal of friendship. It calls for reconciliation, with God and also with ourselves because the effect of sin is to divide us within ourselves.

Failure and renewal
The fact that they became God's people in the desert, and promised to do all that he asked of them, didn't make the people of Israel perfect. Their whole history is the story of a people who were conscious of their special relationship with God, who from time to time broke faith with God and went their own way, and then, recognising their sinfulness, came back once again to the way of God. They were a hard-living and violent people at times. They were stubborn and conceited, but right through the Bible there is the clear sense that God never lost his love for them,

and never broke his promises to them, even when they left him
to follow their own inclinations. The message of God's faithful
love and his forgiveness is to be found, alongside the call to
repentance and conversion, in the preaching of all the prophets.
Isaiah, probably the best known of the prophets, calls on the
people to 'Prepare in the wilderness a way for the Lord'. They
are called to allow the life of God back into the wilderness of
their own sinful hearts. But in the very same passage, Isaiah
gives them a message of hope:

> Console my people, console them,
> says your God.
> Speak to the heart of Jerusalem
> and call to her
> that her time of service is ended,
> that her sin is atoned for. . .
>
> *(Isaiah 40:1-2)*

He tells them that the Lord is calling them back to himself
'like a shepherd feeding his flock, gathering lambs in his arms'.
If, like sheep, they have been foolish and gone their own way,
he has never stopped caring for them.

Jeremiah too preaches a message of conversion and
forgiveness. It is not so much just a question of turning away
from sin, as of turning back to God who has always remained
faithful in his love for them.

> See, the days are coming — it is Yahweh who speaks —
> when I will make a new covenant with the house of Israel,
> but not a covenant like the one I made with their ancestors
> on the day I took them by the hand to bring them out of
> the land of Egypt. They broke that covenant of mine, so
> I had to show them who was master. It is Yahweh who
> speaks. No, this is the covenant I will make with the house
> of Israel when those days arrive — it is Yahweh who speaks.
> Deep within them I will plant my Law, writing it on their
> hearts. Then I will be their God and they will be my people.
> There will be no further need for neighbour to try to teach
> neighbour, or brother to say to brother 'Learn to know
> Yahweh'. No they will all know me, the least no less than
> the greatest — it is Yahweh who speaks — since I will
> forgive their iniquity and never call their sin to mind.
>
> *(Jeremiah 31:31-34)*

So, being God's people is to be understood no longer as just being obedient to a set of laws. To be God's people is to be led by him, to be drawn to him, to respond to him as a lover from the heart. It is only possible because God first makes himself known to his people and shows his own love for them in a way that they can understand. In this way the preaching of the prophets, and particularly this passage from Jeremiah, sets the scene for the coming of Jesus, whose whole purpose is to bring God's people back to him, by coming among them and letting them experience in a deeply personal way the love that God has for each one of them.

John the Baptist, the last of the prophets, prepares the people to hear the good news of God's forgiveness from Jesus, by first of all reminding them that they are sinners, and issuing them with a personal call to conversion. His message was simple and direct! 'Repent, for the kingdom of God is near at hand'. 'If you are repentant, produce the appropriate fruit and do not presume to tell yourselves "we have Abraham for our Father".' When people expressed surprise that Jesus seemed to spend a lot of time in the company of sinners and outcasts, he made it very clear that these were the very people he had come to find. 'It is not those who are well who need a doctor, but those who are sick. I have not come to call the righteous, but sinners to repentance.' (*Luke 5:31-32*). Jesus received a ready response from those who recognised that they were sinners; his real problem was with those who thought they were virtuous. So when Zacchaeus, the little tax-collector, climbed the tree to see Jesus, he was amazed to find that Jesus not only recognised him and called him by name (and not some of the less pleasant names he was often called), but actually wanted to have a meal with him. In reality Zacchaeus was a man who had got caught up in the injustice and dishonesty of the system and had found that he could make a living from it. Too late he had realised that there was more to life than making a profit, especially when it was at the expense of the misery of others. But until he met *Jesus, who was prepared to loved him as he was*, there didn't seem to be any way out. The love of Jesus for this sinner was what made it possible for him to change.

If Zacchaeus was a user, then Mary Magdalene was more accustomed to being used. Most of the men she met had only one interest — what they could get from her. She had no experience of being loved for herself until Jesus came along. Until he came into her life she had been just as hardened as those who made use of her. The love of Jesus taught her how to love and changed the whole course of her life.

To people with small, narrow minds, the law-breaker must always be punished. There is no understanding of repentance and forgiveness. Fortunately the mind of God is neither small nor narrow. The word of Jesus always combines great gentleness with the challenge to the sinner to repent. So when they brought to him the woman who had been caught committing adultery and wanted to have her stoned to death, Jesus asked them who they thought they were to set themselves up as judges. Then, turning to the woman, he said, 'Woman, where are they? Has no one condemned you?' 'No one Sir', she replied. 'Neither do I condemn you', said Jesus, 'go away and sin no more'. He called her to conversion of heart, encouraged her, and forgave her, all in a few words.

When Jesus taught the disciples to pray, he reminded them of the importance of forgiving as well as being forgiven. Before he ascended to heaven he entrusted his followers especially with the mission of reconciliation, telling them to forgive in his name.

> As the Father sent me,
> so am I sending you.
> Receive the Holy Spirit.
> For those whose sins you forgive,
> they are forgiven;
> For those whose sins you retain,
> they are retained.
>
> (*John 20:21,23*)

At a later stage we will look a bit more closely at what this means in practice. For the moment it is enough just to recognise that forgiveness was one of the things which most concerned Jesus in those days after the Resurrection, and that it was his clear intention that future generations should experience his forgiveness in the community, by the power of the Holy Spirit. In exercising the ministry of forgiveness, the Church, his followers, are called to do as he did, both to call people to genuine conversion of heart and to forgive them freely and generously. As with the woman caught committing adultery, so it must be with every sinner. The Church repeats the words of Jesus. 'Does no one condemn you? Neither do I. Go and sin no more.' The sin is always rejected, but never the sinner.

So far, then, we have looked at the idea that God offers us the gift of his love and calls us to find our fulfilment in our friendship with him. Our decision to look for fulfilment in our own way has an effect on the quality of our relationship with God and with one another. In Chapter 2 I will consider the role of Confession in renewing these damaged relationships.

Summary

1. God calls us to find fulfilment in our relationship with him.
2. Sin affects us — not God.
3. Sin is not just a personal thing. It has communal and social dimensions.
4. God's people have never been perfect, so there is a constant call to renewal.
5. This call to renewal of relationship is central to the mission of Jesus.

For reflection

1. Would it usually occur to me that sin inhibits my growth/development as a person?
2. In what sense does my community/country/Church sin socially?
3. Is my image of God that of someone who cares?

2

WHY CONFESSION?

I remember being rather amused once, when a group of teenagers came to me for advice because they had got into trouble with the guards for breaking and entering. They told me how they had broken into a warehouse and taken out a load of electrical equipment, while one of their number kept watch outside. All of a sudden a car had appeared around the corner and pulled up just beside the growing pile of equipment. Two men jumped out, loaded most of the loot into the car and sped off again, before the look-out could do anything. To add insult to injury, it was the young lads who were picked up and questioned. They felt the whole thing was very unfair — not so much the fact that they had been picked up, but the fact that someone else had made off with their hard-earned loot.

It's not unusual for us to notice in others quite clearly the same fault that we are blind to in ourselves. In fact, quite sub-consciously, it is often the faults we have ourselves that we notice and that annoy us most in others. If I'm the selfish type, then I'll be quick to notice the lack of generosity in someone else. If I always have to be in control of things, then I just can't stand the domineering type of individual who always expects things to be done his way. Seeing the sin around me is easy, but facing the reality of sin in myself is another matter and it requires a lot of honesty.

Speaking to his disciples Jesus said:

> If you make my word your home
> You will indeed be my disciples,
> You will learn the truth
> and the truth will make you free.

> *(John 8:31-32)*

The Sacrament of Reconciliation has a lot to do with recognising the truth and accepting it. To begin with there is the truth about myself, good and bad; the kind of person I am;

the fact that I am not all that God has called me to be; the aspects of my life in which there is room for growth and change. This kind of self-understanding comes more easily if a person can get into the habit of reflecting regularly on her life in the light of the Gospel. Reflection is a very different thing from anxious worrying. It is simply a question of taking time and making space to reconsider, in a calm quiet way, events and activities which may have taken place in a more rushed atmosphere or in an un-thought-out way. Reflection can make a person more sensitive to ways of living and attitudes which are good as well as to those which are not so good.

But far more significant than either me or my sins is the truth about God; that, even in my sins, he has not stopped loving me. If our hearts are open to the words of Jesus, and not just to the parts we find easy to accept, then we will understand *both* of these truths and, while a sense of guilt on its own can do nothing for us, the awareness of God's love, *together with* the sense of our own sinfulness, is what encourages us to turn back to God and, literally, sets us free.

'I'm sorry' — 'It's OK'

'What's the point in telling your sins to a priest?', people sometimes ask. 'I just tell God I'm sorry, surely that's enough'. And, true enough, God can forgive sins whenever and however he wants to. Yet, it's interesting to see that, while there has been a decline in the practice of sacramental Confession in recent years, there has been a noticeable increase in the number of people making use of opportunities such as co-counselling in the course of which they tell another person in confidence about their hopes and fears, their failures and their progress in overcoming difficulties. This would seem to suggest that 'confession' in some form responds to a genuine human need.

In the United States, Ron Hubbard, who started out as a science-fiction writer, developed the 'science of Dianetics' as a means by which people could rid themselves of their phobias by re-living childhood and even pre-natal experiences. This was done under the guidance of an 'auditor' — a kind of counsellor. In the early 1950s, recognising the significant tax-advantages involved, Hubbard set up the Church of Scientology and continued to use the 'science of Dianetics' under a religious guise. Recruits to the Church of Scientology were the vulnerable and the bereaved — the casualties of society — many of whom were happy to pay for the privilege of being 'audited' and freed from their 'engrams' (the negative experiences of the past). Scientology is a pseudo-religion but, in its use of auditing, it seems very successfully to have borrowed the idea of confession, and made a lot of money by tapping into the human yearning to be free of the past. Hubbard visited Dublin in 1956 with plans for extending his 'ministry'. These plans were never realised, but the Church of Scientology has recently been established in Belfast. (My sources with regard to Scientology/Dianetics are a person who has had first-hand contact with the movement, and Hubbard's biography, *Bare-Faced Messiah*, by Russell Miller.)

Jesus never actually said that we should always confess our sins in detail. There are other times when we ask God for forgiveness, like at the beginning of Mass, or perhaps if we pray about the successes and failures of the day before going to sleep at night. But at the same time, if we look at what happens in the Gospels, it seems that Jesus understood people's human need to be reconciled on a very personal level. We have already seen how Zacchaeus came to Jesus and admitted that he had dealt unjustly in the collection of taxes, and how he was forgiven and welcomed into the company of Christ's friends. In the parable of the Prodigal Son, Jesus paints the picture of a repentant son coming back and apologising to his father for the way in which he has wasted his inheritance, and shows us the father standing on the doorstep, watching out for his son. Franco Zeffirelli, in his epic film, *Jesus of Nazareth*, has a scene in which Jesus uses this parable both to encourage the repentance of Zacchaeus, and to encourage his own disciples to accept the sincerity of his conversion and be reconciled to the man who had probably ripped off half the people in Galilee.

So the forgiveness of God, as it is portrayed in the Gospels, comes about as the result of a very personal encounter between Jesus and the one who is being forgiven. In entrusting the ministry of forgiveness to his apostles and to those who came after them, Jesus indicated his wish that this opportunity of a personal encounter with a forgiving Saviour should be available to those who would believe in him in future generations also. The two aspects of the Sacrament of Reconciliation which make it a genuine encounter with Jesus Christ (a Sacrament) are my confession of sin with faith in Jesus, and my receiving his forgiveness through the ministry of the Church, represented by the priest.

The truth about myself

To say 'I am a sinner', is a little bit like saying 'I am a member of the human race'. It's true, but not by any means unusual. It's only when I come to terms with the ways in which I am a sinner that the reality often comes home. To many people the idea of confessing individual sins presents difficulties, but often it is only when we are faced with saying it to someone else that we can begin to understand it or to recognise the truth of it for ourselves. So when I can say I caused an accident because I was drunk, or I hurt someone by failing to control my temper, or I broke a promise I made to my wife, my sinfulness takes shape; I have to face up to it and I can't hide from it. It's no longer just a cliché, something everyone says with mock humility like 'I'm really not much of a cook', while all the time waiting for compliments; it is something I know because the evidence is there before me. I am a sinner because of this and that and the other.

Sin is not just a question of things I do or fail to do. The angry word, the stolen money, the work avoided. These are the obvious manifestations of sin but, before the incident, there is the attitude that makes it possible. For example, jealousy or bitterness leads to the unkind word or the broken nose. We really only get to the bottom of sin when we tackle the attitudes that lead to our way of acting. Jesus criticised the Pharisees because, while they kept the law, their hearts were far from God; they had the wrong attitudes (cf Matthew 5:20ff; 15:10-20). (I will take a closer look at the importance of attitude when I discuss the examination of conscience in Chapter 3.)

Then there is the state in which sin leaves my relationship with God and my relationships with others. If any relationship is weakened it is less able to withstand further pressures. A broken promise damages the trust that once existed between two friends. It's not just a once-off event, because the damaged trust makes it less possible to either make or accept promises in the future. On a pre-marriage course, the couples were asked about their attitudes to infidelity in marriage. How would it affect their relationship if one partner was unfaithful? Would they see any possibility of forgiveness, or would it be the end of the marriage? Most of the couples felt that infidelity would place a serious strain

27

on their relationship, and that it would be very difficult to restore the damaged trust.

But the experience of strained or damaged relationships is not restricted to infidelity in marriage. Mrs Jones used to be secretary of a parish committee. At the February meeting last year, Mrs Dunphy said that, with respect, she didn't agree with Mrs Jones' report of what she had said in the minutes of the January meeting. Was Mrs Dunphy suggesting that Mrs Jones was stupid? Was Mrs Jones suggesting that Mrs Dunphy was a liar? It was a long and unpleasant argument over nothing, and at the end of it Mrs Jones announced that she was resigning from the committee. Long after they have both forgotten the phrase in the minutes that started the row, the two women find it impossible to pass one another on the same side of the street. In just the same way, jealousy, a domineering attitude, and pride can damage a good working relationship, and lead to a situation in which two people can no longer face one another.

Tony's situation is different. Over the years he has been taking things home from the stores where he works. At first he found that he could justify it to himself because it was only small things, but then it began to get out of hand. Tony used to drop into the Church quite frequently on his way home from work, but lately he just doesn't feel that he belongs there. The only explanation he can think of is that his dishonesty at work has left his relationship with God strained and weakened.

So sin has a number of different aspects. It begins as an attitude; it is made concrete as an act, a word or a conscious thought, or as a failure to act; and it ends up as a damaged relationship. It is important in confession to try and see the whole picture. Often it is the loss of a sense of direction, experienced as a result of our damaged relationship with God or with our neighbour, that first makes us aware of the wrong attitude which caused the problem in the first place. Sometimes, unfortunately, we become so accustomed to our sinful attitudes and our un-Christian values that we don't feel uncomfortable with them, or, if we do, we don't realise why, and so we do nothing about it.

The truth about God

Recognising that I am a sinner is only one aspect of the Sacrament of Penance. In so far as it is an honest acceptance of the way things are it is a good thing in a limited sense. But to face guilt without the hope of forgiveness is a very drab prospect. To be wrong once can be hard to take. To be wrong many times, and to know it and to be rejected because of it is enough to ruin a person's confidence entirely. If you tell a child often enough that he is a fool, then he begins to believe it, whether it's true or not.

In the Sacrament of Reconciliation, the sinner can face the truth about himself, no matter how bad it may be, only when he faces the truth about God as well. And the truth about God is that he never rejects the sinner, but is always ready to forgive. You don't have to take my word for it, just listen to the word of Jesus:

> . . .what woman with ten drachmas would not, if she lost one, light a lamp and sweep out the house and search thoroughly till she found it? And then, when she had found it, call together her friends and neighbours? 'Rejoice with me', she would say, 'I have found the drachma I lost'. In the same way, I tell you, there is rejoicing among the angels of God over one repentant sinner.
>
> (*Luke 15:8-10*)

The God Jesus reveals to us is not only prepared to forgive the sinner who repents, but is actually out there looking for him. Another well-known image used by Jesus, which tells us the same thing more clearly, is that of the father in the parable of the prodigal son. Who knows how long the wild and wasteful young man had been away from home, but when he returned, expecting to have to bargain with his father in order to be allowed in as a servant, he found the father out on the doorstep looking for him. 'While he was still a long way off, his father saw him and was moved with pity. He ran to the boy, clasped him in his arms and kissed him tenderly' (*Luke 15:20*). God is just that kind of a father who, in the Sacrament of Penance, comes half-way to meet his repentant children.

I believe that it would not be going too far to say that God has forgiven us before we even ask. If there is a problem, it is not his refusal to forgive, but our unreadiness to accept the forgiveness that is always there for us. It is not our sorrow that makes God forgive. It is God's forgiveness that helps us to be sorry and to turn back to him. St Paul expresses this idea very powerfully in his letter to the Romans in which he encourages them not to lose hope:

> . . .this hope is not deceptive, because the love of God has been poured into our hearts by the Holy Spirit which has been given us. We were still helpless when at his appointed moment Christ died for sinful men. It is not easy to die even for a good man — though of course for someone really worthy, a man might be prepared to die — but what proves that God loves us is that Christ died for us while we were still sinners.
>
> (*Romans 5:5-8*)

Too often, our expectations of God are conditioned by our experience of the people around us. We expect not to be forgiven or, if we are forgiven, we expect to have to crawl for it. Boy doesn't quite meet girl. The bus was late. After a row he is forgiven, but his 'sin' is held over in the memory to be used against him at some time in the future. A man serves a six-month prison sentence for petty theft. He doesn't know what got into him. Now that he is out of prison, his debt to society paid, he finds that no one is prepared to give him a second chance. When I'm not too sure that the other person is really willing to forgive, then my expression of sorrow is stunted by the fear that I might be rejected.

Kazuo Ishiguro describes how, in post-war Japan, many of the best men felt that the only way in which they could regain their honour was to commit suicide as an act of public apology. Miyake, a young executive, explains to his prospective father-in-law how the company President died.

> 'Our President clearly felt responsible for certain undertakings we were involved in during the war. Two senior men were already dismissed by the Americans, but our President obviously felt it was not enough. His act was an apology on behalf of us to all the families of those killed in the war.'
>
> 'Why really', I said, 'that seems rather extreme. The world seems to have gone mad. Every day there seems to be a report of someone else killing himself in apology.'
>
> (Kazuo Ishiguro, *An Artist of the Floating World*)

When Archbishop Kevin McNamara was first appointed Bishop of Kerry he chose as his episcopal motto a short statement from the first letter of St John — 'God first loved us.' The message is very simple, but it stands our human way of thinking on its head. We don't have to earn God's love — in fact we couldn't — his love is there for us all the time. All we are asked to do is to allow his love to become a part of us and to influence our own way of living.

Being human, it often helps us if things are made a bit more concrete. A wife knows that her husband loves her, but it helps when he says it occasionally, and when he expresses his affection for her in various ways. We have already seen that, in much the same way, the confession of our sins helps us to come to grips with our sinfulness in a more realistic way. It's the same with forgiveness; even when we know we are probably forgiven, it helps to be told. So, in the Sacrament of Reconciliation, absolution is God's way, not just of forgiving us, but of letting us experience his forgiveness.

Sin is about going away; confession is about returning and reconciliation. If our emphasis is all on sin, Confession can be an anxious and miserable experience. But if we have the balance right we see our sins and God's forgiveness as two parts of the same picture, and our confession can be what it is really meant to be, a celebration of our reconciliation. If there can be great joy in heaven over one sinner who repents, why should our celebration of that repentance be joyless and miserable?

Forgiveness is a community thing
We have grown so used to celebrating the Sacrament of Penance in a dark box, that it is only to be expected that we think of it as something very private and personal. In a certain sense this is true. We can confess our sins with the certainty that our confidentiality will be respected. Nobody else will be told, no matter what the circumstances, that John Murphy stole Mary McCarthy's handbag. But that doesn't mean that our sins are private. Some of our sins affect other people directly. They may know what has happened and who did it, or they may not know who did it, or they may not even know that it has happened. But in so far as my sins harm someone else, they are not private. Sometimes sin seems to be totally personal and unconnected with anyone else, but even then, because it is a pre-occupation with

31

me, and a turning away from others, it can damage my capacity
for love, generosity and commitment.

Even if it seems that my sins have not affected anybody else
directly, they are still the business of the community, because
to be a Christian is to be a member of a community of believers,
and to fail as a Christian is to let the side down. Sometimes it
is not easy even to be sure who has been affected by my sin.
Injustice and violence, especially, can be passed on down the
line for a long time after the original unjust act. The poet John
Donne goes right to the heart of the matter in his poem 'No man
is an Island':

> No man is an island, entire of itself. Every man is a piece
> of the continent, a part of the main. If a clod be washed
> away by the sea, Europe is the less, as well as if a
> promontory were, as well as if a manor of thy friends or
> of thine own were. Any man's death diminishes me,
> because I am involved in mankind. And therefore never
> send to know for whom the bell tolls; it tolls for thee.

If sin is something which concerns the community, this doesn't
mean that everyone in the community has to know about it. What
it does mean is that the community is also concerned with
forgiveness. We saw earlier how Jesus gave his disciples the
responsibility of ministering his forgiveness. He also never tired
of reminding them that they must be prepared to forgive one
another from their hearts on their own behalf. So in the
Sacrament of Penance the sinner asks for and receives not just
the forgiveness of God, but also the forgiveness of the community
for his sins. If, by his sin, he has let the side down, then by
Confession and absolution he is reconciled to the community.

How it all began

In a perfect world there would be no sin, and there would be
no need for the Sacrament of Reconciliation. But this is not a
perfect world and, at a very early stage, the Christian community
began to realise that most of its members would sin at some time
or another and would need to be forgiven. St Paul, St John and
St James all mention the need to avoid sin, and the need to
protect the community from the influence of serious sins (cf 1
Cor 5:1-11). At the same time they encourage the people not

to lose heart if they do sin, but to put their trust in the forgiveness of God. St John says:

> If we say we have no sin in us
> we are deceiving ourselves
> and refusing to admit the truth;
> but if we acknowledge our sins,
> then God who is faithful and just
> will forgive our sins and purify us
> from everything that is wrong.
>
> (*1 John 1:8-9*)

So, in the Christian community, there was always — as Jesus intended — a celebration of forgiveness and reconciliation. When people were baptised and made their commitment to follow Jesus they were forgiven all their past sins, as part of the Sacrament of Baptism. But when a person who was already baptised sinned, he had to do penance and pray for forgiveness. If the sin was a serious one, it had to be confessed to the priest/bishop who would ask the sinner to take on some particular penance as a means of showing sorrow and avoiding further sin. Then, when the penance was done, the sinner, along with any others in the same situation, would be reconciled in a public celebration in the Church and receive absolution from the bishop. In the case of serious sin which required this kind of public penance, the sinner was not allowed to receive Communion until after the penance was done and he had been reconciled. The idea of this was not so much to punish as to bring home to a person that his sin had separated him from God and from the community. Communion is a celebration of our unity with God and with the community and so it would not be appropriate for someone to receive it if he was not at one with God and his fellow Christians.

The practice of Confession was quite strict in another way in the early Church. It was generally understood that there could only be one formal celebration of this Sacrament in a person's lifetime. After that, while a sinner could pray to God, whose forgiveness is never in doubt, he could not be fully reconciled to the community.

It was only in about the seventh century that the practice of Confession became less severe. In Ireland especially, the monks in the monasteries received sinners and prayed with them.

Confession was made in private, and a penance was given, sometimes a period of fasting on bread and water. From this time onwards it became acceptable unofficially that Christians could receive the Sacrament of Penance more than once, although this was still officially frowned upon. Some of the Irish saints, for example St Columban (Colmcille), wrote penitential books outlining the kind of penances that should be asked of sinners for different kinds of sins, in order to help them on the road to healing and restoring their relationship with God and the community. The penances were hard, but they did distinguish between sins of greater or lesser seriousness, and between those which were deliberate and those which were careless. Among the penances suggested in the Penitential of St Columban were the following:

> If any layman has committed theft, that is, has stolen an ox or a horse or a sheep or any beast of his neighbour's, if he has done it once or twice, let him first restore to his neighbour the loss which he has caused, and let him do penance for a hundred and twenty days on bread and water. But if he has made a practice of stealing often, and cannot make restitution, let him do penance for a year and a hundred and twenty days, and further undertake not to repeat it; and thus let him communicate at Easter of the second year, that is, after two years, on condition that, out of his own labour, he first gives alms to the poor,

and

> If any layman has perjured himself, if he did it out of greed, let him sell all his property and give it to the poor, and devote himself wholly to the Lord, and receive the tonsure, bidding farewell to the entire world, and until death let him serve God in a monastery. Yet if he did it, not out of greed, but in fear of death, let him do penance for three years on bread and water as an unarmed exile, and for two more let him refrain from wine and meats and let him communicate after the seventh year.
>
> (Walker, G., *Sancti Columbani Opera*, Dublin, 1957, p.177)

It is worth noting that in both examples the penance, hard as it is, is seen in the light of the penitent's eventual re-integration into the community, through participation in Communion. The penances for priests and monks were more severe because, as leaders of the community, a higher standard was expected of them.

In the end it was accepted that, because of the weakness of human nature, no Christian could be expected to live a life totally free from serious sin, and that the once-only restriction on the celebration of reconcilation would cause even good Christians who sinned occasionally to lose heart.

It was also in the Irish monastic Church that the tradition of confessing less serious sins was first encouraged. It was believed that, while it was possible for these sins to be forgiven just by prayer and penance privately done, to confess them was a worthwhile act of humility and an expression of faith in God's forgiveness. Since that time the Church has always recommended people to confess even their less serious sins, recognising that even these affect the relationship with God and with others.

In any celebration of the Sacrament of Reconciliation, right up to the present time, the same basic elements are always involved — confession of sin, sorrow for sin, forgiveness (absolution) and penance. At different times in the history of the Church different aspects were emphasised more particularly. Sorrow and the intention of avoiding sin in the future is one element that has always been at the centre of the Sacrament of Reconciliation. As we have seen, in the early Church there was considerable emphasis on doing penance. In recent centuries the emphasis was placed more on the importance of a detailed and accurate confession of sins. It is probably fair to say that there is now more emphasis on God's forgiveness than on either penance or confession. In fact, over the last twenty years or so, the Sacrament has gone from being called Confession, to being called the Sacrament of Penance, and from that to being called the Sacrament of Reconciliation. This doesn't mean that sorrow and penance and confession are no longer important, but it just reminds us that what God does in the Sacrament is more important than what we do. In most cases nowadays, of course, the absolution is given first and the penance is done afterwards, so that the sinner doesn't have to spend any long period of time without being reconciled and being free to receive the Sacraments.

Although Confession helps us to appreciate both our sinfulness and our goodness, and gives us the opportunity of celebrating our reconciliation with God and the community, it still holds

35

difficulties for many people. Its not always easy to think of it as a celebration. The next few chapters will look at how we can make the most of our celebration of forgiveness, through using it regularly with trust in God's willingness to forgive, and through being well prepared for it.

Summary
1. Renewal is only made possible by an honest acceptance of the truth.
2. Accepting the reality of sin can be the beginning of new growth only because God loved us first and because 'while we were yet sinners', Christ died for us.
3. As members of a believing community we need to be reconciled to each other as well as to God.
4. We have a human need to experience forgiveness in a personal and tangible way.

For reflection
1. It can sometimes be easy enough to believe in a loving God, but much more difficult to believe that he loves *me*, even with my limitations.
2. Do I approach the Sacrament of Reconciliation as a *celebration*?

3

GETTING ORGANISED

'Bless me Father for I have sinned. It's been . . . . since my last Confession'. Many people still begin their Confession in this way. How often should people go to Confession anyhow? There's no hard and fast rule about the frequency of Confession, but there's no doubt that regular celebration of the Sacrament can be a great help. In the 1950s and 1960s when I was growing up, it was normal enough for people to go to Confession once a fortnight or at least once a month. On average, people tend to go less frequently now. I would be inclined, however, to make a distinction between *frequent* Confession and *regular* Confession.

The fact that people go less frequently to Confession than was the custom some years ago may mean that Confession has become less of a routine. It may mean that people think more about what they are doing and why they are doing it. If this is the case, then it can only be a good thing. On the other hand, there are undoubtedly people who go to Confession very infrequently and yet in a routine manner.

Whether Confession is celebrated once a week or once every six months, it is a good thing to have a regular practice of going to Confession, rather than waiting until something serious crops up. Every relationship needs to be worked at, and even a good one can always be better. Regular celebration of Confession means regular examination of conscience and lifestyle and this helps all of us to be realistic; to be honest with God and with ourselves. Even when there is no serious sin to confess, the celebration of the Sacrament renews and strengthens our relationship with God and our awareness of his love for us. If, on the other hand, we wait until there is something serious to confess, we may find that we don't have quite the same confidence or trust in God's forgiveness. A lot of people recognise that Christmas and Easter are times when Confession is especially appropriate, because they are times when it is important for everyone to be able to participate fully in the religious celebrations, and to have a sense of closeness to God. For that reason, I always like to make my Confession at Christmas and Easter myself. Then, at other times during the year I just know almost instinctively when I need to receive God's forgiveness, because I can feel myself drifting a bit, or getting my priorities wrong. Obviously, as with any friendship, asking forgiveness is especially important when there has been a serious breakdown in the relationship, when there is serious sin.

In a certain sense, the real problem — if there is one — is not the number of weeks from one Confession to the next, but rather the reasons why people sometimes put Confession 'on the long finger'. Sometimes it's just a question of forgetfulness or not getting around to it. But anxiety or uncertainty can also keep people away from the Sacrament, and this is a pity. 'I was afraid to come because it has been so long'. (And so it just got longer and longer.) 'I had a serious sin and I was embarrassed'. (But Confession is about forgiveness and peace, not about blame and recriminations.) 'I wanted to be forgiven, but I wasn't really sure if I had things properly sorted out'. (Then maybe it would have helped to talk to a priest about it.) Probably the most useful thing to remember about Confession is that it is the Sacrament in which God welcomes us, knowing that we are sinners, just as he knew that Zacchaeus, Mary Magdalene, and all the Apostles were sinners.

If there is fear associated with Confession, it stands to reason that part of it has to do with what the priest may think, or what the priest might say. So at this point I'd like to say a few things about the role of the priest and his responsibilities as a confessor.

What will the priest think?
The priest celebrating the Sacrament of Reconciliation has only one real responsibility, and that is to be an instrument of God's forgiveness and peace for the person who comes to Confession. Everything else is secondary. Some people may feel that when they come to Confession they will be judged by the priest and found guilty. But in practice, the role of the priest is not to judge people, but to help them to make their own judgements about themselves and about their actions, in the light of the Gospel. The priest, on the basis of his experience and his training, may make a judgement about what the penitent has told him, in order to help the person to know how serious or otherwise it may have

been. If a young woman confesses that she has had a serious argument with her mother, with whom she is living, the priest may be able to help her by making an objective judgement based on the facts of the situation. If a man confesses that he has received stolen property and is not sure if it is sinful, the priest will be able to tell him that it is and to explain why. But when it comes to judging the person and his relationship with God the priest is not really in a position to judge.

It is only human nature that we sometimes feel a conflict in ourselves about turning away from sin and back to God. It can happen that a person comes to Confession in the hope of making a fresh start and turning back to God, but at the same time is reluctant to take the steps that will make this possible. This could arise especially if a person tends to think of Confession as being mainly about freedom from guilt or, in other words, if the person's approach to the Sacrament is more backward-looking than forward-looking. In a case where a penitent is involved, in an ongoing way, in serious crime or in infidelity to a marriage partner for example, and can see *no way* forward, the priest might think it necessary to ask him to reconsider the situation and to come back again. If, in a situation like this, the priest encourages the penitent to look at other angles or aspects of his situation, this should not be mistaken for 'giving out' as has sometimes been the case. It is not the role of a priest in the confessional to 'give out'.

In the final analysis, there can never be any question of a person being denied God's forgiveness if she is ready to try her best. It must be said that in general people don't come to confession unless they have the intention of turning back to God, even though they might experience difficulty and even failure in doing so to begin with. All God asks of any of us is the willingness to try our best with his help.

While the priest is hearing confessions as the representative of Jesus Christ and of the community, he remains a human being with his own faults and failings. No priest is in any position to think badly of a penitent, because he is only too aware of the fact that he is a sinner himself, and that he too needs forgiveness. In fact, it is in celebrating the Sacrament of Reconciliation that the priest comes up against people at their very best; people who come humbly and sincerely to ask God's forgiveness with faith and good will. I have often been encouraged by the faith and sincerity of people going to Confession, and made to re-examine my own life by the high standards which they set for themselves, even if they don't always reach them. I know that many other priests have had the same experience.

I think people are sometimes afraid that the priest in Confession will be shocked at some particular sin they have to confess. I remember being on retreat as a student, shortly before my ordination, and the retreat director saying that a priest in confession is not that easily shocked, because after the first few months he's not going to hear anything he hasn't heard before. And it's fairly true. The details may vary from person to person, depending on the circumstances, but pride, jealousy, temper, theft and adultery are basically the same from one generation to the next. I spent a month in Italy, working in a parish, the summer after my ordination, and I remember noticing — with a certain amount of relief — that the people there confessed the same kind of sins as they do here in Ireland. Added to that, the main concern of the priest is not the sin but the sinner who has come to be forgiven. The sin itself, however serious, is not beyond the power of God's forgiveness.

One other thing needs to be said about the priest — any priest — hearing Confessions. Because he is human, he will not always be at his best. It may unfortunately happen that when he is not at his best he comes across as impatient or lacking in understanding. It shouldn't happen, but none of us is perfect. Priests, like everyone else, have their human limitations and, while people often ask priests to pray for them, it is sometimes forgotten that the priest in his turn might need the support of the prayers of the community, for God's wisdom and love in exercising his ministry. It solves nothing for a person to allow his understanding or acceptance of God's forgiveness to be spoiled by a bad experience with a priest.

Being my own judge — conscience
People have funny ideas about the meaning of conscience. Even the way we talk about it is strange at times. We say things like: 'I couldn't do that; my conscience would be at me' or 'What does your conscience tell you?' I have an idea that, for a lot of people conscience is almost like an early warning system that goes off when we are about to do something wrong, or like the 'black box flight recorder' which is checked out after a 'plane

crash to see what went wrong. But of course conscience is not something inside us that works independently of us. It is, very simply, the honest judgement that we make about something we are about to do, have done, or should be doing, as to whether it is right or wrong. We measure up what we are about to do against our values and against our overall picture of how we should live. Bishop Donal Murray compares the judgement of conscience with the judgement of a builder following a set of plans:

> In any complex activity, whether it is building a house or knitting a sock, the individual actions are governed by an underlying plan. This plan need not be explicitly in one's mind at every moment. Bricks may be laid or stitches formed with great skill and deftness without constant reference to the final result. Yet the dexterity of the performance counts for nothing unless it serves the overall purpose. (Donal Murray, *Jesus is Lord*, Veritas Publications 1974, p. 60).

When we talk about conscience as the making of a judgement, we are accepting straight away that not all our moral questions will have ready-made answers which we can accept automatically. There will be decisions to be made. Living as a Christian is not just a matter of obeying rules; it is a question of continually trying to grow more like the God in whose image we are made. We cannot assume automatically that a particular way of acting is good just because it is what everyone else does, or because it is allowed by the law of the land. Morality is not just a matter of convention.

We are called to respond to different situations and challenges with generosity and love and not simply to aim at 'scraping a bare pass' by keeping close to the wall set up around us by rules and commandments. The purpose of laws and rules is to help us on our way to becoming what we are called to be as God's people. It is not the laws themselves which are important but the values and the vision which they protect and foster. To take a practical example from everyday life: both the law of God and the law of the state say that we mustn't kill one another. We are obliged to stop at red traffic lights, not because there is anything specially important about red lights but, rather, because life is of value, and can only be protected at busy junctions if there is some system of traffic control. It isn't the law that counts, or the system, but the lives which they protect. In particular situations, however, the protection of life might justify and even require that a driver should go through a red light carefully instead of stopping, e.g. a doctor driving to an emergency case. In the Gospel Jesus pointed out to the Pharisees more than once, that they might have to break the religious laws about the sabbath in situations where they conflicted with God's law of love and justice.

In many cases it is obvious that keeping the rules is the responsible and right thing to do but if, after careful consideration, I follow particular laws, it is not simply because they are laws but because I have judged them to be good laws. Where moral decisions are concerned, there isn't always a law that fits the situation neatly, and in complex situations different laws may often appear to be in conflict. In cases like this it isn't good enough just to throw up our hands in despair because nobody is telling us what we should do, and make no decision at all. We have to seek out the best ways of protecting the values involved and choose a way of acting which is in keeping with our Christian vision of life.

If we believe that God is calling us all to be his people, and to grow increasingly in his likeness, it stands to reason that he reveals his will to us, not just through laws which come from outside but also, as Ezekiel says, by writing his law in our hearts. The Second Vatican Council says:

> Deep within his conscience man discovers a law which he has not laid upon himself but which he must obey. Its voice, ever calling him to love and to do what is good and to avoid evil, tells him inwardly at the right moment: do this, shun that. For man has in his heart a law inscribed by God. His dignity lies in observing this law, and by it he will be judged. (*Gaudium et Spes*, 16).

What this means quite simply is that a person will be judged, not by whether or not he obeyed certain laws and commandments, but by whether he sincerely acted in accordance with what he believed to be right. This doesn't mean that there is no such thing as right and wrong in itself. It simply means that the responsibility rests with each individual to judge what is right or wrong in any particular case. To follow my conscience doesn't mean simply doing what suits me; it means to make a mature judgement, based on all the information available to me. All the things I believe, including especially the Word of God, help to form the judgements I make. Given the promise of Jesus to be with his Church always, the teaching of the Church must always be considered when we come to making our judgements. The belief that we are called to be like Christ is the overall plan against which we judge our individual actions to see if they fit in.

It is only possible to make sound judgements if we have good information. That's what conscience means (taken from the Latin *con scientia,* meaning *with knowledge*). So, in making any judgement, I can't say that I have acted sincerely, or followed my conscience unless I have gone to the trouble to inform myself as fully as possible. Take the example of an industrialist or a farmer who decides that the handiest way of getting rid of some unwanted chemical is to dump it in the stream behind the house. Later on, ten miles down the river, disaster strikes and all the fish in that stretch of the river are killed. The man didn't mean to kill the fish, he didn't know the chemical was so poisonous, but *he should have found out before he dumped it.* Making a mature judgement means asking questions such as 'What is the full significance of this way of acting?' 'Who will be affected and how?' 'Would certain circumstances make it better or worse?' 'Would it make a difference when I do it?'

The *significance of an action* is more than just the consequences that flow from it. Apart from the consequences, I have to consider what the action means; what it is saying. Russia and America have nuclear missiles, which may never have any bad consequences because they might never be used. But they may still be said to be inherently evil because of the fear and the sense of enmity which they create, and because the life-work of so many people is bound up in their manufacture and control. On another level, someone who is sacked unjustly may find a better job immediately. She ends up in a better position, but that doesn't change the moral significance of what has happened or the fact that she has been treated as if she were just some other item of equipment to be disposed of when no longer wanted.

Who will be affected is always an important factor in making a decision. It often happens that, in making decisions, we are somewhat selective about the people whose needs and rights we consider. Somehow it seems less wrong if we steal from strangers.

People who 'don't speak properly' or who live by the roadside are not always considered to be worthy of the same respect or consideration. If the woman ahead of me in the bus queue lives next door, she probably stands a better chance of getting on the bus first. The goalie on the other team is one of *them*, not one of *us*, so if he gets a kick on the ankle it doesn't matter as much. A sincere judgement of conscience will take account of *all* the people who may be affected for better or worse.

It may happen that I make the wrong judgement because I wasn't fully informed through no fault of my own. In such a situation the end result remains the same, but I have honestly acted according to the best information available to me and there is no sin involved. The Vatican Council makes this clear when it states:

> Yet it often happens that conscience goes astray through ignorance which it is unable to avoid, without thereby losing its dignity. This cannot be said of the man who takes little trouble to find out what is true and good, or when conscience is by degrees almost blinded through the habit of committing sin. (*Gaudium et Spes*, 16)

Where there is doubt in my mind as to what I should do, then the obligation to take advice from others who should know is even greater. To follow a doubtful conscience without good reason would be wrong. If, on the other hand, my judgement is clear and I have reached a certain decision of conscience, then I am obliged to follow it.

Ideally conscience goes into action before I decide whether or not to do something. It's not just something that niggles afterwards. A person who is sincere, who prays for wisdom and tries to live by the Gospel will generally have a strong, well-formed conscience, and won't go too far astray without being aware of it. On the other hand, someone who is used to following only his own inclinations and bending the rules to suit himself will have a weak conscience, and will eventually end up finding it very hard to know what is right or wrong at all.

It makes a big difference to our celebration of the Sacrament of Reconciliation if we are well prepared for it, by having spent some time beforehand reviewing the decisions we have made and the way we have lived. This is commonly known as the *examination of conscience*. Most people are probably used to doing this in the church immediately before Confession, but some might find it more prayerful and less rushed at another time or in a different place. It's a pity to find oneself in the 'box' without having had the opportunity to prepare. I would like to devote the next few chapters to this important question of preparation for Confession.

Summary

1. Regular Confession contributes to building up and renewing our relationship with God and with each other.
2. The priest, as a human being, is conscious of his own weakness. As a minister of reconciliation, his priorities are the same as Christ's — to heal and forgive, not to condemn.
3. Genuine sorrow and openness to growth require the making of honest and informed judgements. This is what conscience is about.

For reflection

1. Does Confession mean simply the acknowledgement of sin, or does it mean the acknowledgement of my life as a whole — good and bad?
2. To what extent does my confession involve the making of informed jugements and decisions about the future?

4

USING THE COMMANDMENTS
AS A GUIDE

Breaking the world high-jump record or crossing the Atlantic single-handed must be a terrific experience, the first time round at least. Most of us can only imagine the experience of being the focal point of everyone's attention after winning a gold medal at the Olympic Games — the cheering crowds, the flags, the music and the feeling of deep personal satisfaction. Our smaller achievements fade into the background in the shadow of the bigger ones. Winning a book-token in primary school for being first in the summer exams is important at the time, but is easily forgotten the day you get seven honours in your Leaving or graduate with a PhD. Even our major achievements lose a certain amount of their excitement and novelty if they are constantly repeated. So, crossing the Atlantic single-handed for the fifth time is not quite the same thing, and most people with a spirit of adventure have to search around for new challenges to keep the excitement alive.

Any sin commited for the first time probably has the capacity to shock the sinner. Many children find the temptation of loose change lying on the mantelpiece almost impossible to resist. The first time they take it, they can scarcely believe what they have done. After a while, if they keep it up, they can develop a system and become quite accustomed to it, and somehow it doesn't seem so bad anymore, especially when it is compared to other 'more serious' things like stealing from a shop. Even the more serious sins can lose their capacity to shock the sinner, if they are committed often enough. Embezzlement from the company, or adultery with the woman down the road are unthinkable before they happen, shocking the first time, when we think of what we have done, and become gradually more commonplace the more they are repeated.

Added to this there is the problem that at times we can confuse sin with getting caught and when, after the first few times, nothing happens, we begin to feel that it's all right. A young man came to confession in a very agitated state, and confessed that he had embezzled money from his employer; a thing which he had never done before. When he thought about it afterwards he half expected to be struck dead or at least to find that some of his projects had gone wrong 'as a punishment', and he couldn't wait to get to confession. Sometimes the fear of being caught can help us to stay on 'the straight and narrow'. On the other hand, if we commit the same sin repeatedly and nothing happens, the fear of being caught wears a bit thin.

So what I am saying is that the awareness that a particular sin is serious, or the fear of 'being caught' can sometimes make it very easy to know what needs to be confessed and forgiven. But this is not always the case, because we overlook our more common sins more easily, and often find ways of justifying them to ourselves. For this reason it is useful to have some objective set of guidelines by which to judge ourselves. Since we are God's people, the obvious thing is to examine our lives in the light of his word and his commandments.

The Ten Commandments of the Old Testament, given to Moses on Mount Sinai, appear at first sight to be very straight-forward. They outline what is required of God's people in their relationship with God and in their relationships with each other. But if we are to use them in our examination of conscience we need to go beyond just a superficial look at them and try to come to grips with the important values which they are designed to protect. The remainder of this chapter will tease out the real meaning of the Ten Commandments for Christian living in the twentieth century, and we will try to discover, not just what they forbid us to do, but what they encourage and require us to do and to be.

1. I am the Lord your God. You shall not have false gods before me.

It's easy to overlook the importance of this commandment. We're all aware of how Moses discovered the people of Israel worshipping a golden calf when he came down from Mount Sinai after his encounter with God. But golden calves and idol worship are gone out of fashion, at least in modern western society. But hold on a minute — this commandment is not really about the worship of idols at all, it is about the respect and the priority that is due to God because he is *our God*. So to begin with, it is worth asking if we have an awareness of God as our God. Where does he come on our list of priorities? If he takes second place, to what does he take it? St Augustine, who came to God only after trying out nearly everything else, said 'Our hearts were made for you, O God, and they shall never rest until they rest in you'. Jesus himself, when speaking to his disciples, said 'Where your treasure is, there will your heart be also', (*Matthew 6:21*). Is the attraction of wealth or social status, or the lust for power the focal point of all my efforts and thoughts? Does the whole world revolve around me? In a certain sense the first commandment is the one which gives meaning to all the rest, because if I give priority to God, then I will keep his commandments; but if I put something else before him as my real priority, then this and not God will dictate how I act in my dealings with others as well. A man who is obsessed with diamonds or with heroin will be ruled by diamonds or heroin, as the case may be. And when these rule, the seventh commandment changes as well to: 'You may steal, in order to fulfil the demands of your addiction'. This is just one example of how a disordered relationship with God puts everything else out of order as well.

2. You shall not take the name of the Lord your God in vain.
If my experience is anything to go by, most people confess to taking the Lord's name in vain (or 'calling down the Lord's name' as they say in Dublin) at some stage or other. But what do they mean? In most cases they mean using the name of God as a swear word in order to express their impatience or their anger. A lot of the time it is a quite unconscious habit, and certainly isn't intended to show disrespect for God. In some parts of the country, using the Lord's name in this way is as common as talking about the weather. Among the people of Israel God's name was held to be so sacred that it was never spoken by the ordinary people, and only by the priests on very solemn occasions. Instead God was referred to as The Holy One or in some other similar way. Perhaps they carried it a bit too far, but it certainly makes sense that God's name should not be reduced to the level of a swear-word.

But there is a far more significant meaning to this commandment which is often forgotten. There is one particular situation in which we call on the name of God, and that is when we take an oath. 'I swear by Almighty God that the evidence that I shall give shall be the truth, the whole truth and nothing but the truth'. In an oath, God is called as witness to the truth of what I say. The ultimate insult would be to call him as witness to a lie. Here again, we are reminded that quite frequently the same thing is a sin against God and against our neighbour. The eighth commandment talks about perjury as it affects the person against whom the false evidence is given, while the second reminds us that perjury offends God who is called as witness to it.

The members of some professions are expected to take oaths, e.g. doctors — to respect life; the military — to defend the state; the police and the judiciary — to uphold the law. In the beginning, the taking of an oath requires that someone intends to keep it. The real crisis comes when the soldier is called upon, in the name of the state, to murder innocent civilians, or when the judge is called upon to preside over the administration of unjust laws. In such a case a person best fulfils an oath by doing what is good, even if such action conflicts with orders or with the law.

While priests, religious, and married people are not bound by oaths, they do take vows in the presence of God which give a special significance to what they undertake to do, by invoking God's name.

3. Remember to keep holy the sabbath day.

The original idea of the sabbath day among the Jews of the Old Testament was to have one day in seven to celebrate their freedom as God's people. When they were slaves in Egypt, they had no rights and were only allowed to rest so that they could do more work, but God brought them out of Egypt and they became free people. So the sabbath day became for them a symbol of their freedom and an occasion for celebrating the Lord's goodness. According to the Book of Genesis God rested when creation was finished, not because he was tired, but because his work was done. Likewise the people of Israel rested. As time went on the Jews got a bit tangled up in laws, and rules about laws, so that they sometimes lost sight of the real reason for the commandments in the first place. We hear Jesus on many occasions in the Gospel reminding the people that the law about the sabbath is not intended to place a burden on people but rather to set them free. The fact that they are to rest from work is not to be used as an excuse for ignoring the needs of a neighbour in difficulty. In fact the Sabbath day is a very good day to do things which help to free others from their difficulties and to relieve them of their burdens, because in that way we share with them the gift of freedom which we have as God's people.

As Christians, the special day which we celebrate is Sunday, the day of the Lord's Resurrection; the day the Holy Spirit came as God's special gift to his people. The day is different, but the idea is much the same; we are God's people and he has set us free, not from being slaves in Egypt, but from being slaves to sin. We celebrate our freedom through our participation in the Mass (Eucharist means thanksgiving), and through abstaining from what the Church calls 'unnecessary servile work'. We will look briefly at each of these ideas.

In the early centuries after Jesus there was no such thing as an obligation to attend Mass on Sundays. It was just understood that anyone who was serious about being a follower of Jesus Christ would naturally want to gather together with the rest of the community to celebrate their faith, to give thanks and to receive the Eucharist, and Sunday was the obvious day to do it. The Church only made attendance at Mass obligatory in order to remind people who were inclined to be a bit careless about it that this was an important part of being a Christian, and something which Jesus himself asked his followers to do.

Of course, just getting along with the minimum is not a very positive attitude, and when we examine our conscience about our attendance at Sunday Mass it is important to take account of what it is really meant to be — a community prayer. Anyone can have difficulty with parking or an emergency nappy-change from time to time, but in general we must recognise that arriving after Mass has started is a distraction to others as well as meaning that we lose out on part of the liturgy ourselves. It is amazing how easy it is to fall into the habit of arriving late Sunday after Sunday. In practice it is quite difficult to arrive in at the last minute, or after Mass has started, and then try to focus one's attention on what is going on, so people who are habitually late will easily find after a while that they lose interest altogether.

One other thing to consider before making our Confession is how we actually spend the time during Mass. Do we join in the prayers of the community, do we pray quietly, or do we just sit there like vegetables waiting for the Mass to end? Communion is an integral part of the celebration of Mass — where does it fit into my participation? A priest might examine his conscience on how well he has prepared for the celebration of Mass, whether he leads the celebration in a dignified manner, and whether his homily was genuinely the proper presentation of God's word. Some people have particular difficulties about their participation in the Mass and we will have a closer look at some of these in a later chapter.

The other aspect of the Church's teaching about the Third Commandment is the obligation to abstain from unnecessary servile work. When this law of the Church was first introduced it was because the Church recognised that, while ladies and gentlemen of leisure had all the time in the world for whatever they wanted to do, many working people had no free day; no day to remember especially the Lord's goodness, and no day to spend a little time with their families and to rest and renew themselves. For them, work was a dehumanising thing. For this reason the Church's teaching about resting on Sundays is not just a question of making sure that everyone has the time to go to Mass and to reflect on their relationship with God through prayer or reading. It is also a reminder that, while work is important, every worker has a need and an obligation to set aside some time for others, especially his family and those in need, and for himself. Work must not become slavery, nor must it become an obsession.

People sometimes worry about doing any work on Sunday at all, and it is worth remembering that the obligation refers to 'unnecessary servile work' only. Some work will always be necessary on Sundays such as the work of people in transport and communications and in the emergency services, as well as the hotel, catering and leisure industries. The work of parents seems to go on all the time. For people who must work on Sundays the obligation remains to allow sufficient time for their families and for their own human needs on some other day. Servile work means simply the work we do in order to earn a living. This varies from one person to another, so that what might be servile work for one person is relaxation for another. Some people worry about working in their gardens on Sunday, but for most people this is not servile work. For most people painting landscapes is a hobby and a relaxation, but for a professional artist it would be servile work.

If we take to heart the idea that part of the reason for the Sabbath rest is to allow us the opportunity to enrich the quality of our family lives, then it is worth considering in our examination of conscience whether we actually devote a reasonable amount of that free time to our families, or whether an undue amount of it is spent on our own particular interests.

4. Honour your father and your mother.

One of my regular customers in the confessional for a number of years was a lovely old woman who, among other things, always confessed that she had been disobedient. Maybe it was just a habit she grew into as a child of mentioning the same sin in every Confession, or perhaps she had a little more insight into the fourth commandment than many people have.

Respect for parents, and for the elderly generally, is part and parcel of many religious traditions apart from Judaism and Christianity. Because this commandment talks about how we should treat our mother and father, there is a danger that we might think it is just for children and so pass on without giving it much more thought. But actually the commandment says nothing about honouring parents up to the age of eighteen or twenty-one. The first thing we need to notice is that the commandment talks about honour and not obedience. In other words, it is about having the appropriate attitude towards our parents whatever age we are.

For children, the appropriate attitude towards parents includes obedience as well as respect. Parents cannot fulfil their responsibilities of caring for and educating their children unless their authority is accepted. As young people grow older and become more mature, it is important for both them and their parents to recognise that the relationship between them is changing gradually. Although parents can require obedience of their children until they become adults themselves, the emphasis should increasingly be on a relationship of co-operation. So for a seventeen-year-old it would be helpful during the examination of conscience to go beyond the question of disobedience, and honestly to answer the question. 'Have I co-operated with my parents in fulfilling their responsbilities towards me, and have I participated in a reasonable and generous way in the life of the family, or have I allowed my increasing interests and commitments take precedence over everything else?'

Adults, of course, are not expected to obey their parents, but that is not to say that they are relieved of the obligation to honour them. The examination of conscience for adults might include questions such as whether I have any interest in my parents' material well-being, whether I spend any time with them, and whether I am prepared to accept that no matter how old I may be myself they have a need and a right to be concerned about me. To honour someone doesn't mean always accepting that he is right, but it does imply respect for his values and judgements even when they differ from my own.

In the culture of the Jewish people, particularly at the time of the Covenant, the system of civil and religious authority was largely patriarchal and both orthodoxy and social stability depended to a great extent on the honour and obedience shown to parents. In the more complex social structure of the modern world, it would be reasonable to suggest that the Fourth Commandment includes the obligation of having the appropriate attitude towards all those who are, legitimately, in positions of responsibility. If we look a little more closely at this idea, we can easily see that anyone who has a responsibility needs to be able to exercise authority of even a limited kind in order to fulfil that responsibility. So governments, Church leaders, teachers, librarians, bus conductors, gas inspectors and a whole host of other people have authority to a greater or lesser extent over those whom they are called to serve. In the process of preparation for Confession it may be helpful to include the following questions in the examination of conscience. Do I find it hard to accept the authority of others? Am I a superior type? Do I feel that the rules can always be bent for me, that they are 'only there to be broken'? In so far as I have authority myself, do I exercise it justly and in a spirit of service, with respect for people rather than for institutions? Do I recognise that all authority is subject to the law of God?

5. You shall not kill.

This is another of the commandments which we might be inclined to pass over with just a quick glance. After all, if you kill someone you'll know all about it, and it doesn't seem to be the kind of thing that a person would have any doubts about, as to whether it was right or wrong. It is helpful if we think a bit about what this commandment is meant to protect. It is really a commandment about respect for life, which requires us not simply to avoid killing, but to avoid any action which would damage the quality of either our own lives or the lives of others. From a very practical point of view, it is neither realistic nor morally acceptable to expect someone to respect my life or my quality of life, if I am not prepared to respect his. For a Christian, the knowledge that every person is made in God's image and loved by God is still more reason to respect her life and dignity.

Murder is probably the first thing that comes to mind when we think of the Fifth Commandment, but murder is not the only way of killing somebody. Dangerous driving or driving under the influence of alcohol may result in the death of another person. Even though the end result may not have been intended, it is important in an examination of conscience to be realistic about the degree to which I may have been responsible for what happened. The same applies if someone dies as a result of my carelessness or negligence at work. In some cases it may seem that self-defence makes it necessary to kill, but this could only ever be justified if it was the only possible means of defence, and to choose freely to kill another person is never acceptable. As a person, I cannot be the arbiter of another person's right to life, no matter what he or she has done.

Killing quite often begins with a wrong attitude — an attitude which may be encouraged by people who don't actually do the killing. Sectarian murder is not just the sin of the individual who pulls the trigger; it is also the sin of those who deliver provocative speeches, those who contribute to the sectarian divide, those who supply the weapons, those who provide assistance to the one who kills and those who aprove of or rejoice in the killing. Similarly those who encourage a driver to 'have one more' or who condone his getting into a car which he is incapable of controlling, must accept some of the responsibility when an accident occurs. It is a well known fact that abortion is often the result of pressure from family, boyfriend or husband, rather than the freely chosen decision of an expectant mother. Those who contribute to the decision cannot avoid taking responsibility for it, nor indeed can those who participate in the procedure in the course of their work.

In some cases it is only through good fortune that someone is not killed. But to freely take the risk of killing or causing serious injury is in itself an offence against human life. It is as if we were to say that life wasn't really so important that we should take special care of it.

Many courses of action damage the quality of life and show a lack of the respect which is due to human life. Violence of all kinds, angry words and actions, the misuse of power or authority all fall into this category. Employers might examine themselves as to whether they provide a healthy working environment for their employees, and landlords as to whether their accommodation reaches a standard which is apropriate to the dignity of human living. The abuse of alcohol or drugs damages the quality of the user's own life because, apart from any physical harm it may do, it also runs the risk of making him temporarily lose control of his own decisions and actions. Added to this, his abuse of drink or drugs may be the cause of his doing harm or causing hurt to someone else.

In the Sermon on the Mount, Jesus urged his followers to adopt a higher standard than just the observance of the minimum that the law required. 'You have learnt how it was said to our ancestors: "You must not kill", but I say this to you; anyone who is angry with his brother will answer for it before the court. . . .' (*Matthew 5:21-22*). Holding grudges, refusing to forgive, creating bad feeling — all offend the spirit of the fifth commandment, and risk going further.

Respect for life and for its quality is also a matter of public responsibility. In a world where people starve to death, or live in refugee camps, in a country where people are forced to live on the side of the road, each person, as well as being responsible for his or her own attitudes and prejudices, shares some responsibility for the attitudes and prejudices of society as a whole.

So when we come to the fifth commandment in our examination of conscience we might ask:

> Did I kill anyone, either deliberately or through carelessness or neglect?
> Did I participate in killing or in acts of violence?
> Could my attitudes or prejudices have contributed to death or injury?
> Have I given way to violent anger?
> Does an attitude of respect for life and its quality influence my dealings with others? What do I do to contribute to the development of attitudes which respect life?

6. You shall not commit adultery.

Sex is only one aspect of the Sixth Commandment, but its the one most people think of first. If by any chance you have just opened the book at this page, let me just say that I think this commandment is a very important one, and one that causes great concern to many people, but it is no more or less important than many of the other commandments. Adultery, in the strict sense of the word, means sexual intercourse between a married person and someone else who is not that person's marriage partner. When you think of it in this sense, it becomes easier to see that the sixth commandment is about fidelity in marriage, respect for the family, and the appropriate use of sex.

The difference between marriage and many other relationships is that in marriage a man and woman make an exclusive commitment to each other, 'for better for worse, for richer for poorer, in sickness and in health' all the days of their life. Sexual intercourse is the expression of that total commitment. What does intercourse mean when it takes place between a married person and someone other than the marriage partner? It means that the commitment to the marriage partner is taken back and offered to someone else instead. It just isn't possible to be totally committed to two people.

But being faithful means a lot more than just not sleeping with someone other than one's marriage partner. It means spending time together, listening as well as talking, being sensitive to the needs of one's partner, and not expecting more of the partner than he or she is able to give at any particular time. The words of St Paul, often used in the marriage ceremony really describe the meaning of fidelity:

> Love is always patient and kind; it is never jealous; love is never boastful or conceited; it is never rude or selfish; it does not take offence and is not resentful. Love takes no pleasure in other people's sins, but delights in the truth; it is always ready to excuse, to trust, to hope, and to endure whatever comes. Love never comes to an end.

In practice then, fidelity means not just staying together, but creating the conditions which make it possible for love and commitment to grow. One of the characters in Albert Camus' novel, *The Plague,* describes sadly how his marriage fell apart for want of attention more than anything else.

You get married, you go on loving a bit longer, you work. And you work so hard that it makes you forget to love. As the head of the office where Grand was employed hadn't kept his promise, Jeanne too had to work outside. . . . Owing largely to fatigue, he gradually lost grip of himself, had less and less to say, and failed to keep alive the feeling in his wife that she was loved.

The examination of conscience for a husband or wife should include some thought about what they may have done or failed to do which has either contributed to or damaged the quality of their relationship. Am I always reading the paper/looking at TV/out playing golf/out at Bingo? Do I pull my weight when there are things to be done? Do I say thanks/notice any special things my partner does/pay a compliment?

Not every couple is blessed with children. For those who are, having a family involves many additional responsibilities. One of these responsibilities is to provide, as far as possible, for a secure family environment in which their children can grow up and learn the meaning of love. This is an added reason for fidelity and for the effort which is needed to keep love alive and growing. Anything which offends against fidelity or damages love takes the risk of hurting the children too.

Again, as far as the children are concerned, the fidelity of their parents means a lot more than just having them both under the one roof. It means having the confidence that they love one another, and seeing this love in everyday living. It means that parents share with their children all that is important to themselves. We provide for the material well-being of our children; we see that they lack nothing that they need. Do we spend time with them/talk to them about the things which interest and concern them/share with them our values and our faith?

Along with fidelity in marriage and respect for the family, the sixth commandment is concerned with the appropriate use of the gift of sexuality. In the past it was widely believed that 'sexual sins' were automatically more serious than other sins, because sexuality has such an important significance for human life and relationships. In some ways the wheel seems to have turned full circle and many people seem to believe that as far as sex is concerned 'anything goes'. The truth is somewhere in between. It may be true that the Church, or some individual priests, have tended to place too great an emphasis on sexuality, but my own experience in the confessional would suggest that for a great many people, both married and single, sex is an aspect of life which has great personal significance; which can be a source of happiness or sorrow, loneliness or companionship; and which has great potential both for building up and for destroying relationships, depending on how it is used.

Sex is about love and about life-giving. It is important for life-giving that it should always be in the context of love. It is equally important that love should not be inward-looking but should reach out to others, which it does especially when it gives life. In this context it is worth mentioning that many people experience anxiety because of difficulties with masturbation which, they can see, does not fit into this understanding of sexuality. It is something which most people can deal with successfully even though it may take time. Anxiety doesn't help, but can actually make it more difficult to deal with this or any other area of weakness. (The problem of anxiety is dealt with in more detail in Chapter 5.)

Some years ago, when I was teaching religion at a school, the question of sexual intercourse outside marriage was raised. One sixteen-year-old asked the obvious question: 'If I love my girl-friend and respect her, and she doesn't mind, then why can't we make love?' I tried to answer the question by explaining that intercourse is an expression of commitment. The class didn't seem to be convinced. A few years later, the same young man (then about twenty-two) told me that a week or so before going on his holidays with his girlfriend he had been up in her house, and her brothers started a discussion about sex before marriage. Obviously they were interested to know what kind of person their sister was going on holidays with. He had told them that he didn't believe in sex outside marriage, because there was no guarantee that they wouldn't change their minds at a later stage and end the relationship. I like to think that what he said was the same as the answer I had tried to give a few years earlier, only he put it a lot more simply.

Sexual intercourse is about two becoming one. It is about a meeting of minds and about shared understanding and the coming together of two persons, not just two bodies. By its very nature it says 'I give myself fully to you. Nothing will come between us.' If that kind of commitment is not yet there in the relationship, then intercourse is really saying something that is not true. It is not being honest about the state of the realtionship. If there is something preventing a couple from getting married, for example, age/doubts about their relationship/other commitments/lack of even the basic resources, then they are not yet ready to make that commitment to each other, much as they might wish to. There are, of course, times when everything works out, but to enter into a full sexual relationship without the appropriate commitment, apart from not being 'authentic' as the Americans say, runs the risk of eventually hurting one's partner very deeply. We don't usually risk hurting someone we love.

I know that many couples, not all of them young, experience difficulties in deciding just what level of sexual expression is appropriate for their relationship, and then sticking with that decision. This is something I will return to in a later chapter.

The other aspect of sexuality is its life-giving character. Many people seem to be confused about the Church's teaching about family planning. Certainly the Church does not teach that every sexual act should result in pregnancy, or that couples should have as many children as possible. The right and the responsibility of family planning rests with the couple, and the size and spacing of the family which is best for one couple will not necesarily be best for another. What the Church teaches, quite simply, is that intercourse must always be open to life. To put it another way, pregnancy must not be prevented by any artificial method, which changes the meaning of sexuality by taking away its capacity to give life. The teaching of the Church is not about the number of children in a family, it is about the attitude of a couple towards their children and towards their sexuality. The Church recognises too, that family planning is not a woman's responsibility alone, but the responsibility of a couple. In fact, the use of natural methods of family planning is only possible where there is co-operation and mutual respect between a husband and wife. Experience in the confessional would suggest that many of the problems encountered in the area of family planning are the result of an inability on the part of a couple to talk together about their sexuality and their fertility.

In the area of sexuality, the way we act depends to a large extent on the attitudes we have. If we see sex as a means of enjoyment without responsibility then we will more easily tend to use sex in an irresponsible way, either in or outside of marriage. When one looks on the other partner as a person who needs to be loved, respected and understood, rather than hurt, abandoned or used, this will influence the way one acts.

Young people especially, because they are particularly aware of their sexuality and that of the opposite sex, will at times experience difficulty with their thoughts and feelings. Both young men and young women frequently confess to having had 'bad thoughts'. The problem is not that we are aware of sex, or think about it or even talk about it, but that we do so in an inappropriate way. It is not sex that is wrong, but sometimes the attitudes that we have cheapen it, and degrade others in the process. A thought that flashes into my mind is not a sin because it is the product of my imagination, but to nourish an inappropriate thought is 'a different kettle of fish'. No one can isolate himself completely from the influences around him, but our attitudes are largely formed by what we see and hear around us, and for this reason it is important to be selective about the conversations we enter into, the things we read and the films we watch, again not because sex is bad but because it is good and can sometimes be cheapened and degraded.

In the examination of conscience in relation to sexuality a person might ask: Do I have appropriate attitudes towards sexuality? Do I understand that to be a woman or a man is more than just to be a body? Do I try to own/control/possess other people? Do I think more of my sexual rights than my responsibilities? Is the way I act with my partner appropriate to the kind of relationship we have and the level of our commitment? Am I selfish/caring/honest? Do I promote inappropriate attitudes to sexuality, e.g. through writing, conversation, advertising?

7. You shall not steal
Some of the boys were missing things — pens, books, keys and all the other bits and pieces that schoolboys carry around or keep in their desks. Eventually Paul was caught in the act and brought to the headmaster's office. The headmaster asked him why he stole from the others in the class, and pointed out to him that there was a commandment against stealing. Paul put on a bit of bravado and claimed he didn't believe in commandments anyway. So the headmaster suggested that they agree to suspend the seventh commandment for a week or so and see how things worked out. Over the next few days Paul began to notice that

some of his own things were missing — his football boots, his watch and a few other things besides. He went to the office to report that his things had been taken, and was at first surprised, then furious, when he found that the headmaster had them all in the drawer of his desk. It wasn't fair — but then — the seventh commandment had been suspended for the week, and stealing was allowed.

The seventh commandment requires us to respect the property of others. Society works largely on trust, even though our experience tells us that this trust is often betrayed. But it is only because we can expect most people to respect our property that it is possible for us to go away and leave it all day. If we all had to stay at home and mind our property then society would grind to a halt. This commandment is a very practical example of the application of the golden rule 'Do to others as you would that they should do to you.'

We tend to have stereotyped images of what stealing is. It is breaking into someone's house and taking things. It is robbing a bank. It is knocking over old ladies and taking their handbags. These are all sinful of course, but they are only the visible edge of sin where the seventh commandment is concerned. The Irish Bishops in their pastoral letter, *The Work of Justice,* point out that some forms of dishonesty and injustice have become socially acceptable, and that often the only 'sin' is the disgrace and the embarrassment of being caught.

> There are many ways of stealing; and some of them are quite sophisticated and can be practised by so-called sophisticated people. Things like over-charging, profiteer-ing, selling inferior goods, turning in inferior workmanship, drawing money for work that is not done, living beyond one's means while not meeting one's bills — people do not think of these things as stealing; but stealing is what they are. Stealing can sometimes pass itself off as cuteness or cleverness or as 'beating the system'. It can pretend to be business drive, getting ahead. But the new ways of cheating others are just as much stealing as the old ways; and the proper name for those that practise them is still 'thief'. (n. 46, p. 22).

It is amazing how we sometimes manage to justify our breaches of the seventh commandment. The best of the lot is what might be called the 'Robin Hood syndrome'. We've all heard people attempting to justify dishonesty on the basis that the person or organisation which is cheated can well afford it anyway. 'The supermarkets are covered against shop-lifting', Harry told me one day in school, 'it doesn't matter to them.' But who pays the insurance? Companies and public bodies suffer, I think, from being 'faceless'. If I can't actually see who it is I am robbing, then I can convince myself more easily that isn't really wrong. But the simple fact remains — if it isn't mine, then it belongs to somebody else.

Of course some people don't take the risk of being caught stealing. They receive stolen property from others. 'It's hard to turn down a good bargain at the door Father, and sure if I don't buy it someone else will only get it anyway.' But buying stolen property at knock-down prices is all part of the process, and if there was no market for it, a lot of it wouldn't be stolen in the first place.

Living beyond our means is something we hear a lot about in a time of recession. But the one who lives beyond his means is not always the one who ends up paying for it. When Mary gets a bigger slice of a smaller cake, then it is everyone else's slice that becomes smaller as a result. Some may end up getting none at all. It is possible to steal from someone without actually taking something concrete. If my greed, laziness or carelessness at work makes the company less secure, it makes the jobs of my colleagues less secure, and deprives other potential employees of the right to a job. Many other dishonest practices on-the-job, as well as cheating employers, damage the business in such a way as to affect all who work in it. These practices include taking things home from work for my own use, and wasting time and resources at work. The little I take, or the small amount of time I waste may not seem that important, but when it is multiplied by every day of the year and every person on the job from tea-boy to manager, then it can mount up. The fact that I work somewhere doesn't mean that it is less wrong to steal there; actually the fact that I work there means that I am in a position of trust, and to take advantage of that trust really makes the matter more serious.

Justice is not just a matter for individuals. Companies, multinational corporations and nations must accept responsibility for any way in which they contribute to injustice or inequity. The payment of a fair weekly wage is not a matter of charity, but a question of justice. The practice of paying people less because they need the job badly is unjust, and is particularly common in times of high unemployment. Young workers and contract workers are particularly prone to being exploited, often receive less pay, are deprived of benefits as a result of the way their working hours are arranged, and frequently enjoy considerably less security. If my company, or my government department is responsible in any way for the fact that people live in poverty, or indeed die from it, for the sake of profit-margins or cost-savings, or just out of sheer lack of consideration, then that too is a matter for the examination of conscience.

Nobody likes paying tax, and most of us feel that we are over-taxed. If we are, part of the reason is that some of us don't carry our fair share of the burden. Tax fiddles may appear to be just a question of beating the system, but we depend on that same system for all our public services, so when we are dishonest about tax we really end up cheating each other. The same applies to dishonesty in relation to public funds in any other way. The Irish bishops say:

> An attitude has been growing up in this country in recent years that problems of morality and conscience simply do not arise when it is a question of public money. This attitude is immoral and unChristian'' (*The Work of Justice*, n. 90, p. 47).

Dishonesty with regard to public funds is all the worse because, when there is a shortage of funds, it is always the poorer sectors of the population who suffer as a result of cut-backs in various public services such as health, education, transport and others.

The seventh commandment is about respect for property, so it is not just stealing that is at issue, but damage to the property of others. The obvious example of damage to property is deliberate vandalism. But many people who wouldn't consider themselves vandals are careless about the property of others, especially borrowed property. Again, public property often suffers more from vandalism and carelessness because it doesn't obviously belong to anybody in particular.

There are so many implications arising from the seventh commandment that we could go on discussing it a lot longer if there were space. In examining my conscience I might ask myself:

'Have I stolen anything — big or small?' 'Have I deprived others in any way because of my greed or selfishness?' 'Am I honest and prompt in paying what I owe — public and private?' 'Have I respected the property of others or have I damaged it?' 'If I have broken this commandment, have I made restitution?' (I will look at the obligations of restitution at a later stage.)

8. You shall not bear false witness.

We have already seen how perjury (swearing falsely in court) offends against God, because he is called as a witness to a lie. Obviously perjury also offends against justice, and may lead,to the innocent being condemned. There is no cure for perjury other than to go back and tell the truth.

But it isn't only in court that lies hurt others. To take away another person's character by telling lies about him can damage his career prospects and affect his relationships with his family and friends. Lies like this are often motivated by jealousy or revenge. Once again it is wrong attitudes that are the root of the problem.

Far more subtle and more damaging in some ways are the half-truths and exaggerations that build up a false picture on a basis of truth. Some of the gossip that goes on in offices and over garden walls is harmless enough, but some of it can be quite vicious. The truth can be twisted and presented in a way that suits the teller and the listener. People's motives can be questioned and suspicions raised, and the story grows with the telling. The idea that gossip is a female sin is just a piece of gossip spread by men who are just as good at it when the occasion arises. People working in the media, because they can reach so wide a population with their reports, need to be especially conscious of their obligation to present an objectively truthful view of issues and events. The damage done to other people's characters by means of careless or malicious talk is well-illustrated by the story of one woman's confession (at least it was a woman in the version I heard). It seems that the poor woman confessed that she had told lies about her neighbour, and was genuinely sorry about it. For her penance, the priest told her to take a bag of feathers and go up the nearest mountain. On the top of the mountain she was to shake out the feathers. Then she was to come back to him the following week. When she came back and told the priest that she had done as he asked, he said 'Now off you go back up the mountain and collect the feathers again.' 'Sure father', she said, 'God knows where they are now.' 'Yes', said he, 'and the same applies to the lies you told about your neighbour.' A hard lesson certainly, but a good illustration all the same.

The members of some professions have special responsibilities when it comes to information. Doctors, lawyers, priests and journalists are among those who, because of the special relationship of trust which they have with their clients, are obliged, as well as respecting the truth, to respect the confidentiality of any information they receive in the course of their professional dealings with their clients. Careless talk can cost lives, create embarrassment, and leave people in positions of vulnerability.

'Do not judge and you will not be judged', Jesus said, 'because the judgements you give are the judgements you will get, and the amount you measure out is the amount you will be given. Why do you observe the splinter in your brother's eye and never notice the plank in your own?' (*Matthew 7:1-3*). Even without speaking lies and half truths about people, we can bear false witness against them in our hearts by the judgements we make. How easy it is to make a judgement about someone and to be mistaken. How simple it is to move from judging the crime to judging the one who commits it, even though we know how hard it is to see clearly into another person's heart. To make a judgement about *something another person does* is often a necessary thing, but when I begin to judge *the person*, I am in danger of forming a wrong attitude towards him, and I leave myself open to being judged by the same standards. Few of us are really ready for that. 'If there is one of you who has not sinned, let him be the first to throw a stone at her'. (*John 8:7*)

9/10. You shall not covet.

The sin involved in breaking the ninth and tenth commandments is really the same, the problem of evil intention. The original text of the Ten Commandments in the Book of Exodus and in Deuteronomy runs the two commandments together:

> You shall not covet your neighbour's house. You shall not covet your neighbour's wife, or his servant, man or woman, or his ox, or his donkey, or anything that is his.
>
> (*Exodus 20:17*).

This particular format is not very flattering to wives who are lumped in along with all the rest of a man's property. We need to remember that for the people of the Old Testament the wife was considered a kind of property and had more obligations than privileges. This idea is not compatible with Christianity, though it has taken a long time to die out. In any event, probably in order to make a distinction between the wife and the property, the Catholic Church has always tended to divide this commandments into two: 'You shall not covet your neighbour's wife' *and* 'you shall not covet your neighbour's goods'.

To covet means more than just wishful thinking. It includes jealousy, and evil intention of depriving someone else of what is rightfully hers if at all possible. Jealousy is the initial wrong attitude; it isn't so much the fact of being less than satisfied with what I have myself, but the fact that I begrudge someone else what she has, her good looks, her academic achievements, her job, etc. Jealousy can lead on to covetousness, which is a more concrete attitude; it could be described as the planning stage, when I set my mind to getting something even if it means doing wrong. Whether I am successful or not doesn't really enter into the question; it is a matter of what I intend.

To covet my neighbour's goods, then, is to place my own desire for wealth, property or position before the rights of my neighbour. It amounts to saying 'What I want is what is important; you don't count.' In this way covetousness is blind to the other person as an individual with needs, hopes and fears. It is this blindness which makes it possible for thieves to steal and murderers to kill, for witnesses to lie and for nations to go to war. So the commandment against covetousness is not just something tagged on at the end. It is a further reminder that sin begins with wrong attitudes and evil intentions, and that these must be 'nipped in the bud'.

To covet my neighbour's wife (or my neighbour's husband) is different in one very important way. If I set out to take as my own someone else's partner in marriage, I set out to destroy a relationship. It may be a good healthy relationship, or one whch is already weakened by difficulties which the couple have had themselves. In this situation I offend, not just the one whose partner is coveted, but also the partner, because they have made a mutual commitment in which I have no right to interfere. In a moment of weakness, or of disillusionment with marriage, 'my neighbour's wife' may well be a willing accomplice but, irrespective of that, the fact that I contribute to destroying whatever they have between them, or fail to recognise the exclusivity of their marriage, is my sin. Once again, it is a question of what I want taking priority over everything else.

The Commandments have their limitations

The Ten Commandments are the word of God, and they are as valid now as they were when they were first given. But the Commandments are God's word seen through the eyes of the people of Israel long before the coming of Jesus Christ who reveals God's word in its fullness. The purpose of this chapter has been to examine the commandments in the light of the Gospel of Jesus who said that he came not to abolish the law but to fulfil and complete it. Taken in isolation from the teaching of Jesus, the Commandments would be an inadequate tool for a Christian examination of conscience. Some people prefer other approaches to the examination of conscience. We will look briefly at some of these, and at other aspects of preparation for Confession in Chapter 5.

5

FROM ANOTHER ANGLE

In the Gospel the whole law of the Old Testament is summed up as love of God and love of neighbour. The trouble with love is that it sounds good, but it isn't always that easy to make it concrete or to pin it down. For many Christians the best expression of the law of love is the Sermon on the Mount. It could provide a very positive alternative to the Ten Commandments as an aid to the examination of conscience.

> Seeing the crowds, he went up on the hill. There he sat down and was joined by his disciples. Then he began to speak. This is what he taught them:
>
> How happy are the poor in Spirit:
> theirs is the kingdom of heaven.
>
> Happy the gentle:
> they shall have the earth for their heritage.
>
> Happy those who mourn:
> they shall be comforted.
>
> Happy those who hunger and thirst for what is right:
> they shall be satisfied.
>
> Happy the merciful:
> they shall have mercy shown them.
>
> Happy the pure in heart:
> they shall see God.
>
> Happy the peace-makers:
> they shall be called sons of God.
>
> Happy those who are persecuted in the cause of right:
> theirs is the kingdom of heaven.
>
> Happy are you when people abuse you and persecute you and speak all kinds of calumny against you on my account. Rejoice and be glad, for your reward will be great in heaven; this is how they persecuted the prophets before you.
>
> (*Matthew 5:1-12*)

In this passage 'happiness' doesn't necessarily mean that the good disciple of Jesus will always feel great about it and be on top of her form. It means, rather, that she will reach fulfilment and be counted among the blessed.

Am I poor in spirit, then, or is my heart full of envy, jealousy and greed? To be poor in spirit has nothing to do with what I actually own; it means the ability to possess things without being possessed by them. It is the difference between living for money and having money in order to live.

Am I gentle, or do I dominate and control people by means of force, fast-talking, or sarcasm? Am I an 'operator'?

Am I really concerned with what is right, to the extent that I would put myself out; or am I more concerned with what will work and what I can get away with?

Is mercy one of my qualities, or do I make people suffer for their mistakes? Am I willing to forgive?

What are my motives? Am I pure in heart, or am I motivated by pride? Do I see the good in things and in people, or do I see only the opportunity to exploit?

Am I a peace-maker, or a trouble-maker? Do I seek reconciliation with God and with others on my own behalf? Do I attempt to bring together people who are at loggerheads, or do I add fuel to the fire and then stand back and watch the fun?

Do I stick to my principles, and remain faithful to the Gospel in spite of the criticism or ridicule it may bring, or am I more inclined to go with crowd?

Jesus calls his disciples 'the salt of the earth' and 'the light of the world'. Am I full of zest and enthusiasm as a member of the Church, or am I mediocre and passive? Do I hide the light of God's love, keeping it just for myself, or am I happy to be an instrument of his love to others?

In his play, *Murder in the Cathedral*, T.S. Eliot has a good description of mediocrity and passivity. It takes the form of a prayer for forgiveness spoken by the women of Canterbury, because they recognise that so much evil goes on around them daily, culminating in the murder of their Archbishop. They are basically good, ordinary people, but they have done nothing and said nothing.

> Forgive us, O Lord, we acknowledge ourselves as type of the common man.

Of the men and women who shut the door and sit by the
fire;
Who fear the blessing of God, the loneliness of the night
of God, the surrender required, the deprivation inflicted;
Who fear the injustice of men less than the justice of God;
Who fear the hand at the window, the fire in the thatch,
the fist in the tavern, the push into the canal,
Less than we fear the love of God.

We acknowledge our trespass, our weakness, our fault; we
acknowledge
That the sin of the world is upon our heads; that the blood
of the martyrs and the agony of the saints is upon our heads.

Finally, how are my attitudes? Am I angry, resentful and
seeking revenge, or understanding and forgiving? Am I given
to lust and exploitation or to respect and appreciation? Jesus
finishes his sermon:

You have learnt how it was said: You must love your
neighbour and hate your enemy. But I say this to you: love
your enemies and pray for those who persecute you; in this
way you will be sons of your Father in heaven, for he causes
his sun to rise on bad men as well as good, and his rain
to fall on honest and dishonest men alike. For if you love
those who love you, what right have you to claim any credit?
Even the tax collectors do as much, do they not? And if
you save your greetings for your brothers, are you doing
anything exceptional? Even the pagans do as much, do they
not? You must therefore be perfect, just as your heavenly
Father is perfect.

(Matthew 5:43-48)

The law of the Spirit
Before his death Jesus promised his disciples that he would send
them the Holy Spirit to teach them the fullness of the truth. When
they received the Holy Spirit, the disciples found that they were
able to live according to the teaching of Jesus, in love and mutual
respect, and to preach the Gospel honestly and without fear of
the consequences. They recognised that the change in them was
not something which they had achieved on their own, but was
only possible because Jesus was with them through his Spirit
as he had promised. Even then, of course, it was possible for

the disciples to resist the Holy Spirit, and to go their own way. So, when it came to sharing their possessions, some of them cheated the community. Some of them continued to live in the old way, allowing prejudice, greed, bitterness and wrangling, idolatry and sexual abuse to ruin their relationships with God and with each other.

All of us who are baptised and confirmed have received the same Holy Spirit as the first disciples did. His strength, guidance and wisdom are ours for the asking. But sometimes we expect the Spirit to direct us in spite of ourselves. We resist the promptings of the Spirit and still hope that everything will be all right in the end.

When all is said and done, the purpose of the examination of conscience is to assess honestly the extent to which we live in conformity with the Spirit of Jesus. In his Letter to the Galatians, St Paul has a passage which could form a good basis for a simple examination of conscience.

> Let me put it like this: if you are guided by the Spirit you will be in no danger of yielding to self indulgence, since self-indulgence is the opposite of the Spirit, the Spirit is totally against such a thing, and it is precisely because the two are so opposed that you do not always carry out your good intentions. If you are led by the Spirit, no law can touch you. When self-indulgence is at work the results are obvious; fornication, gross indecency and sexual irresponsibility; idolatry and sorcery; feuds and wrangling, jealousy, bad temper and quarrels; disagreements, factions, envy, drunkenness, orgies and similar things. I warn you now, as I warned you before: those who behave like this will not inherit the kingdom of God. What the Spirit brings is very different: love, joy, peace, patience, kindness, goodness, trustfulness, gentleness and self-control.
>
> *(Galatians 5:16-22)*

Which of the fruits of self-indulgence do I produce, and which of the fruits of the Spirit?

Life situations
It is always important for the examination of conscience to be positive and forward looking, and not just a depressing review of all that is wrong in my life. For this reason it is important,

not just to recognise my sin, but also to acknowledge the areas of my life in which God's Spirit is really making some progress with the development of right attitudes and virtues. It is also important to be able to think in terms of what needs to be changed in the future so that I can grow closer to God. It is sometimes helpful to divide my life up into its different aspects in order to see just where the good and bad attitudes are most prevalent. I could consider the way I have lived the Gospel in my work situation, in my home, in my relationships with my friends, in my relationship with strangers and casual acquaintances, and in my relationships with God. If I am lacking in generosity, is this something which arises only with my family, or is it right across the board? If I tend to dismiss people as fools, do I act like this towards my friends or only towards the people with whom I work?

If I discover that a particular attitude arises right across the board, then I know that the development of a new contrary attitude is called for. If a wrong attitude seems to arise only in one particular area of my life, then it seems that there is something about my approach to that particular situation or the relationships it involves, which needs changing.

Tell me the worst

I sometimes wonder if doctors are ever called 'Father', because I've been called 'Doctor' more than once in the confessional. Maybe it's an indication that people often expect the same kind of treatment from a priest as they get from a doctor; first an examination, then a diagnosis, and then a prescription, all leading up to a cure. But it isn't the same at all. The priest can only help the penitent with the examination and the diagnosis. He can sometimes suggest various remedies which can help a person to avoid sinning in the future, and the 'cure' — the forgiveness he gives — is from God.

So, when someone wants to know how bad his sin is, he is expecting a diagnosis which the priest is not in a position to give for certain. Whether a sin is mortal (i.e. alienates me completely from God) or venial (leaves me less close to God than I was before), depends on a number of factors, most of which are known only to the sinner himself. To use the traditional language, a sin is mortal when it involves *grievous (serious) matter*, and is committed with *full knowledge* and *full consent*. 'Father, is it a mortal sin to miss Mass on Sunday?' In reply to that, all I can say is that it's a fairly serious thing not to join with the rest of the community in celebrating the Eucharist as Jesus asked, because it can isolate a person from the community and from the gifts of God's Word and Sacraments. But I can't decide to what extent Mary fully understood the implications of what she was doing and freely chose to offend God by going against his wishes. Did she realise it was Sunday? Did she forget to go because a friend called? Did she fail to go, even though she wanted to, because she hadn't the courage of her convictions when she was away with her friends? Was she sick? Is she going through a bad patch in relation to her faith; experiencing doubts and discouragement?

I would be a mistake to assume that every sin is mortal, which a person with a very sensitive conscience might be inclined to do. Equally it would be a mistake to assume that most sins are only venial. The main purpose of the examination of conscience is not just to come up with a list of sins, but to try and assess the quality of my present relationship with God. For this reason it is important to be able to judge my actions and omissions from the point of view of the effect which they have had on the relationship. It would be hypocritical, of course, to use this kind of distinction in order to get away with as much as possible short of a mortal sin because, in the final analysis, any sin is an offence against God and shouldn't be taken for granted.

Does it involve grievous matter? To begin with, I might ask myself whether this way of acting was particularly mentioned as being serious in the teaching of Jesus in the Gospel as, for example, was the sin of giving scandal or bad example to the young. Is the significance of the sin such that it is in total conflict with the law of love (e.g. betrayal of a marriage partner)? How serious are the consequences of the sin for others (e.g. murder, perjury) or for myself? Is it the kind of sin that leads inevitably to the risk of further sin as, for example, armed robbery may lead to murder?

Did I commit this sin with full knowledge? Did I know what I was doing, and did I understand the significance of it? Did I understand the consequences that might, and probably would, arise from it? Some people, because of their age, experience or professional training might be expected to have a better understanding. A doctor or a pharmacist engaged in drug-pushing would be doing so with a much fuller knowledge than many other people. If a small shopkeeper went out of business because his customers didn't pay their bills regularly, the responsibility would be greater for those customers who knew that he was in financial difficulties than for those who didn't. When young people first began 'joy-riding' they might honestly have said that they never realised the sorrow and loss of life that might result from it. But now its consequences are widely known, and this knowledge places a greater responsibility on people. In the final analysis, the priest can't tell to what extent a person understood the significance of his action or his failure to act. It is a matter for the honesty of the individual.

Full consent to a sin doesn't always mean that I have deliberately chosen to reject God. It may mean that I have deliberately gone against his commandments, knowing that it was wrong, and hoping that everything will work out all right in the end. We would like to hold on to God's friendship, but on our own terms, and we convince ourselves that he won't mind really. Full consent is probably the most difficult thing to be sure of, because it involves human freedom, and it is not always easy to assess to what extent a person acted freely.

Generally speaking, when I choose to do something of my own accord, while I am of sound mind, I have given full consent. There are some things which may affect a person's choices in certain situations with the result that their consent may not be full or free. Among the factors which may affect consent in this way are excessive pressure from others, habit, addiction, emotional disturbance, and fear. Again, this is something which the priest can only know at second hand, and it rests with the person coming to confession to make an honest judgement about the extent to which his sin involved full consent. Even where freedom is limited by habit or addiction, there remains the responsibility to do whatever is possible to overcome the habit, even though that may take time and effort. This is something which will be examined in greater depth in a later chapter.

The influence of alcohol or drugs sometimes limits freedom to the extent that a person is not fully aware of what is happening and doesn't fully consent to it. This is sometimes made an excuse for acting or failing to act. 'Paul beat up his wife the other night, and she ended up in hospital with serious head injuries. But it wasn't really his fault, it was the night of the office party and he had a few jars taken. He didn't really know what he was doing.' 'Mary was suffering from a hangover after the weekend so she didn't get to work this morning. She just rang in and took a sick day.' We can fool ourselves very easily when it comes to questions like this. Alcohol limits my freedom, so I'm not really responsible for what I do. But if I know that alcohol beyond a certain amount makes me incapable and affects my judgement, with possible serious consequences, it is my responsibility to make sure that I don't go beyond the amount of alcohol that I can take without getting into that condition. It's a question of exercising my freedom of consent while I still have it.

A person who is mentally deficient or handicapped may in some cases be capable of full or reasonably full knowledge, but never of full consent. For this reason the parents or relatives of such a person need never be concerned about the state of his relationship with God. He lacks, by definition, the capacity to reject God or his commandments with full freedom.

Anxiety and guilt

The practice of confessing past sins, which have already been forgiven in confession, used to be encouraged as an act of humility, especially when a person had committed no particular sins since the last confession. To remember that I have sinned in the past may be a helpful thing if the memory makes it easier for me to avoid sin now or in the future, but it is important to remember that *once a sin has been confessed sincerely and absolution has been received, it has been forgiven once and for all.* Some people, especially older people, tend to be very concerned about the sins of their youth. Perhaps the gradual approach of old age makes people more aware of the importance of being close to God, and more afraid of losing him. But his love and his power to forgive are greater than all our sins, and he always keeps his word.

It is common to hear people say these days that guilt feelings only come as a result of the way we have been brought up, the Church we belong to, and the environment we live in. But that would be to suggest that there was no such thing as a real sin at all, no possibility of being genuinely guilty. When I do something that I know is wrong, it is quite right that I should have a sense of guilt. Where the problem arises is when guilt takes over and makes me lose hope in the possibility of being forgiven. Guilt should only act as a starter; something to move me towards a change of heart and towards seeking God's forgiveness. If I become obsessed with my own guilt, my attention is so caught up with the failures of the past, that I have no energy to devote towards living the gospel in the present. Obsessive guilt may be a sign of lack of trust in God. It may also in a strange kind of way, be a sign of pride, because I have failed in my own estimation and I cannot forgive myself. I thought I was better and now I am disillusioned. The first step towards accepting forgiveness is to accept the reality of my sin, and to recognise that if God can take me as I am, then I should be able to accept myself. If we look at the Scriptures, we find that most of those who were closest to God and to Jesus sinned, many of them seriously. Moses refused to take God at his word. David committed adultery with the wife of one of his soldiers and then had the soldier killed in order to cover his tracks. Peter betrayed Jesus within hours of the Last Supper. In a sense there was only one real difference between Peter and Judas; both were trusted Apostles, both were loved by Jesus and both betrayed him. From the Gospel it is clear that both Peter and Judas were sorry, but *only Peter trusted Jesus enough to come back and ask for forgiveness.*

Anxiety about the future can be a problem as well, especially for someone who has been struggling with sin for some time and trying to love God better. Progress is sometimes two steps forward and one step back. The well known Jesuit spiritual writer, Anthony de Mello, has a piece which has a word of hope for people who are anxious. It is entitled 'Don't change'.

> I was a neurotic for years. I was anxious and depressed and selfish. Everyone kept telling me to change. I resented them, and I agreed with them, and I wanted to change, but simply couldn't, no matter how hard I tried. What hurt the most was that, like the others, my best friend kept insisting that I change. So I felt powerless and trapped.
>
> Then one day he said to me, 'Don't change. I love you just as you are'. These words were music to my ears: 'Don't change. I love you just as you are'. I relaxed. I came alive. And suddenly I changed. Now I know that I couldn't really change until I found someone who would love me whether I changed or not.
>
> Is this how you love me, God?
>
> (*The Song of the Bird*)

A young man confessed to a regular problem with masturbation. It was something he wanted to overcome. He felt that there might have been some excuse for it when he was younger, but now in his twenties he felt that it was weak and selfish, and that it didn't reflect the true meaning of his sexuality. It turned out that his difficulty was a habit that went back a number of years, and it was especially a problem for him when he was lonely or anxious. He was always trying to overcome it, but whenever it happened he felt discouraged and anxious, and lost the will to try again. The trouble with a habit of this kind is that it takes longer to get out of than it did to get into. So when we set unrealistic goals for ourselves we become easily discouraged whenever we fail. So the answer to my young friend's problem was partly to be found in patience, and in doing his best each day, without worrying about what would happen tomorrow or next week, and partly in believing that God still loved him. Anxiety about the possible sins of tomorrow only diverts our attention from the challenge of living the Gospel today. Anxiety about one particular sinful habit can divert my attention from other areas of my life which are equally important. In fact, the best way of overcoming a habitual sin is often to concentrate on building up the opposite virtue, rather than worrying all the time about the sin itself, (e.g. developing a habit of generosity, kindness or helpfulness is often the best way of overcoming selfishness). About anxiety, Jesus had the following to say:

> So do not worry about tomorrow: tomorrow will take care of itself. Each day has enough trouble of its own.
>
> *(Matthew 6:33-34)*

To say, 'Do not be anxious about tomorrow', doesn't mean 'Don't bother about it'. It just means 'Take the necessary steps today and leave tomorrow in God's hands until it comes'.

Scruples

Mary was an intelligent professional woman with a good husband and family. But, for her, Confession was a terrible ordeal. It wasn't that she was a notorious sinner, but that she suffered badly from scruples. To begin with, even though she knew that some sins were more serious than others, she had herself convinced that most if not all of her sins were mortal sins. She knew that she was the main judge of her own sinfulness, and she couldn't bring herself to take the risk of deciding that some of her sins were not serious. She was highly aware of all the possible consequences, however unlikely, of her actions. If she came across a collection in the street for some charity, she would convince herself that her failure to contribute something would cause terrible deprivation for some poor person. Where full knowledge was concerned, she always felt that she should have known and should have foreseen. She believed that all her actions and failures might well be seen by God to be deliberate.

Added to this, Mary was terribly afraid that, in her Confession, she might forget and leave something out, or present it in a way that the priest would misunderstand and that as a result she wouldn't be properly forgiven. For people like her Confession can be a major cause of anxiety and the source of very little peace or awareness of God's love.

Anyone who is worried by scruples should begin by mentioning this to the priest in Confession. It is quite common for people who have a difficulty with scruples to 'shop around' from one priest to another, mainly because they find it hard to trust either their own judgement or that of anyone else. But it is better for a scrupulous person to go to the same priest on a regular basis, so that the priest can become more familiar with the penitent's situation, and be in a better position to provide whatever help is needed. For someone like Mary, the best thing is to fix a definite frequency for Confession, e.g. once a month, and not to come more often. In between times, she could make a simple, honest Act of Contrition. When she came to Confession she should mention only those sins which she was certain were serious. Given that she has difficulty in making judgements, it might well be best for her to go to the same priest each time so that she can develop a sense of trust and be helped, over a period of time, to deal with her anxiety. Her main emphasis in the Sacrament should be on the love and mercy of God for all sinners. For other advice she should ask the priest's help, preferably outside of Confession, so that the Sacrament can remain for her mainly a celebration of God's forgiveness.

Summary
1. Confession is not just about the wrong I have done, but also about the good I have not done.
2. No other human being is as well-placed as I am to assess the state of my relationship with God, or the way it is affected by my lifestyle.
3. Worrying about the past or the future is no help in dealing with the present.

For reflection
1. Is my pre-occupation primarily with keeping 'on the right side of the tracks' or do I think always in terms of the possibility of growth in holiness and towards perfection?

6

CELEBRATING FORGIVENESS

When I was about six years of age, I made my first Confession. We were carefully prepared for it at school, right down to being given examples of the kind of things we should tell. In my first Confession, I confessed to having stolen sixpence from my mother's purse, because that was one of the examples we had been given and I couldn't think of anything else to say. Like the rest of my class, I had been told exactly what to do and when to do it, and I suppose having some kind of structure made it easier. At least things worked out better for me than for Jackie, the young boy in Frank O'Connor's short story, 'First Confession', who was scared stiff going into the box.

> It was pitch dark and I couldn't see the priest or anything else. Then I really began to be frightened. In the darkness it was a matter between God and me, and He had all the odds. He knew what my intentions were before I even started; I had no chance. All I had ever been told about Confession got mixed up in my mind, and I knelt to one wall and said 'Bless me Father for I have sinned, this is my first Confession'. I waited for a few minutes, but nothing happened, so I tried it on the other wall. Nothing happened there either. He had me spotted all right'.

The celebration of forgiveness is not meant to be just a formula of words, but a personal encounter with a loving God, through the ministry of the priest. For that reason we need never be afraid to make it personal, to make our Confession and express our sorrow in our own way. At the same time, most of us find it helpful to know what is expected of us, and this is probably particularly true for someone who hasn't been to confession for some time. With this in mind, I have included, at the end of the book, a 'sample Confession', which may be of use to some readers (see page 106).

There are four main aspects to any celebration of the Sacrament of Reconciliation. These are confession, expression of sorrow, absolution, penance. It will be helpful to look more closely at these, to see what they mean and how they are related.

The confession of sin

As we have seen in an earlier chapter, the main idea behind the confession of sins is that I recognise the closeness or distance in my relationship with God and the fact that I am a sinner who needs forgiveness. God doesn't need to be told that I have done this or that, and the priest is not interested in keeping it all on file. The confession of individual sins is really a question of saying 'I know that I am a sinner because I have done this and failed to do that'.

So what exactly am I expected to do? The requirements as regards Confession are outlined in the *Code of Canon Law*.

> The faithful are bound to confess, in kind and in number, all grave sins committed after Baptism, of which after careful examination of conscience they are aware, which have not yet been directly pardoned by the keys of the Church, and which have not been confessed in an individual Confession. The faithful are recommended to confess also venial sins'.

The Church also requires that Catholics confess their grave sins at least once a year. This is to ensure that nobody remains excluded from the life of the community and the celebration of the Sacraments for long periods, as a result of putting Confession 'on the long finger'.

If I deliberately keep back a serious sin in Confession, I'm not being completely honest with myself; I'm not facing the reality of my sin. It may be that this particular area of my life is one with which I need special help. On the other hand, the Church has always recognised that the situation can arise where a person finds it simply impossible, at least for the time being, to confess a particular sin, because he just can't bring himself to talk about it. (This is a different thing from saying that he would prefer not to have to talk about it.) In such a situation it is sufficient that the penitent is genuinely sorry, and he can mention the sin in Confession at some other time if it becomes possible for him to do so. In the meantime he might go so far as to ask forgiveness 'for the sins I have confessed, and for one which I am not at present able to confess'. The judgement about

81

what ought to be, or can be, confessed depends entirely on the sincerity of the penitent.

The idea of confessing the frequency of a particular sin is partly to help the priest to assess whether there are some areas in which the penitent may experience particular difficulties. Once again, the important thing is not really this sin or that sin, but the way in which these sins may be affecting a person's relationship with God. The fact that a person falls into sin regularly in one particular way may suggest a weakness in that area, and the need for some special help or guidance in the confessional.

Memory, or rather the lack of it, can be a terrible nuisance for some people, especially older people. There is never any need to worry about sins which may have been forgotten. The obligation is only to confess those serious sins of which I am aware after a careful examination of conscience. Any sin which is genuinely overlooked and not confessed is nonetheless forgiven, because I have honestly confessed my sinfulness as I am aware of it at the time.

Strictly speaking, there is no obligation to confess venial or less-serious sins. All the same, any sin is a distancing from God and no sin however small should be taken too lightly. Actually, if you think about it, the smaller sins of impatience and lack of charity, especially if they happen frequently, can chip away at our human relationships, and so at our relationship with God. Sins which are less serious in themselves may set the trend towards more serious ones. If a man is honest in small things, he will be trusted with more important things. It is helpful, then, to confess venial sin, and to acknowledge that even in the absence of grave sin, there is always room for growth in our relationship with God.

Penance

Coming home from Confession as a child, my mother would often ask me, 'Well, what did you get?' In those days the penance seemed to be always three Our Fathers or three Hail Marys. The trouble with penance is that a lot of people mix it up with punishment. They are two very different things. Who ever heard of asking people to say prayers as a punishment? It certainly wouldn't be a very Christian approach to prayer. And anyway the whole idea of forgiveness is the renewal of friendship, and punishment just doesn't enter into it. So what is penance all about?

The Rite of Penance tells us that after the confession of sin,

> . . .the priest proposes an act of penance which the penitent accepts to make satisfaction for sin and to amend his life. The act of penance shall serve, not only to make up for the past but also to help him begin a new life and provide him with an antidote to weakness. As far as possible the penance should correspond to the seriousness and nature of the sins. This act of penance may suitably take the form of prayer, self-denial, and especially service of one's neighbour and works of mercy. These will underline the fact that sin and its forgiveness have a social aspect.
>
> (n. 46)

There are a number of important points here. Firstly the priest 'proposes'; he doesn't 'impose'. Whatever act of penance the penitent does it is freely accepted as an expression of sorrow. It might be a good idea if the penance were decided by the priest and the penitent together, so that it truly becomes an expression of the penitent's willingness to turn away from sin and back to God. Obviously the penitent is more familiar with his own life situation and may be able to suggest more realistic and appropriate penances. The other thing we notice is that the penance has two purposes, to attempt to put right the damage done by sin, and to set out on the road to renewal of the relationship with God.

In some cases the damage done by sin is not that obvious. The person offended against may not even realise it, and it may even do more harm than good to bring it to her attention. If I have said something which is damaging to the character of another person and she doesn't know, what good is to be served by telling her? There would be more good involved in taking back what I have said if possible, or trying to find something good to say which may help to restore the balance. In other cases the damage is very clear, as for example when I take something that doesn't belong to me. There is only one way of repairing the damage in this kind of situation and that is by replacing what was taken, or its value. The obligation of *restitution,* where possible, always applies to sin against the seventh commandment. It may not be possible for a person to repay what was taken all at once and in this case it should be done over a period of time. There is no obligation on the person who has stolen to reveal his identity to the person he has offended, if this is not already known.

In other cases the damage done by sin cannot be repaired, and all the sinner can do is to try in some way to make up the loss or the hurt to the person who is offended. He in his turn is called upon, in the Spirit of the Gospel, to forgive as God forgives and not to expect the sinner to do the impossible:

> Be compassionate as your Father is compassionate. Do not judge, and you will not be judged yourselves; do not condemn, and you will not be condemned yourselves; grant pardon, and you will be pardoned.
>
> *(Luke 6:36-37)*

We cannot actually injure God or take anything from him. He is offended by sin in the sense that his love is rejected. All he wants for the sinner is a change of heart; a return to the path of life.

> Am I likely to take pleasure in the death of a wicked man — it is the Lord Yahweh who speaks — and not prefer to see him renounce his wickedness and live?
>
> *(Ezekiel 18:23)*

The other important purpose of penance is this renewal of the relationship with God, through turning away from sin and trying to live more completely according to the Gospel. This involves the breaking down of wrong attitudes and habits and the development of good ones. Penance can help us to do this by setting definite goals for us to aim at. If a young person confessed that he had been thoughtless and selfish and caused arguments at home, I might suggest to him that he would look closely at his involvement in the family and select some way of being more a part of the family, e.g. taking on some kind of responsibility in the home. The advantage of this would not be simply that he was doing some good, but that he might develop more of an awareness of the needs of the other family members and a greater sense of belonging and shared responsibility.

If a woman confessed to having taken too much to drink on a number of occasions, I would suggest for her penance that she should do two things. Firstly she should work out what quantity of alcohol is appropriate for her, and decide to limit herself to that whenever she is drinking. It is not quite so easy for some people to make this kind of judgement after they have already had a few drinks. Secondly, I would suggest to her that she make some sacrifice in the area of drink, which she would decide herself, and perhaps make some contribution to a charity.

The same kind of approach could be applied to whatever sin is confessed. Ideally, I think the penance should always include some prayer as well as some action; prayer as a means of renewing the damaged relationship with God, and to ask for wisdom, strength and perseverance. The Our Father is a very appropriate prayer in this context, because in it we acknowledge God as Father, pray that his will may be done, ask for the help that we need, and are reminded to forgive as we have been forgiven. But one Our Father prayed reflectively is worth more than a half-dozen rushed ones. The aim of the exercise is not to 'heap up empty phrases', but to unite ourselves in prayer with the Father.

Situations which increase the risk of sin
Part of being willing to renew one's life and to live in accordance with the Gospel is the willingness to avoid situations which have consistently led to sin in the past. If going away for the weekend with a particular group of friends has usually meant missing Sunday Mass because they aren't interested, then perhaps I should consider not going in future. If doing business with a particular supplier presents the opportunity of a money-saving fiddle which is hard to refuse, then I should consider dealing somewhere else, where the opportunity doesn't arise. Young couples sometimes find that certain situations make it especially difficult for them to exercise self-control in sexual matters; out of mutual love and respect they should avoid situations in which they feel that there is undue risk.

It is important, however, to be realistic about occasions of sin. We live in a world where good and bad exist side by side, and it isn't possible for us to isolate ourselves from every source of temptation. This is why the development of good, Christian attitudes and habits is the best defence against sin. Where the home or the workplace is the occasion of sin, then avoiding it is usually not a realistic possibility. A person working in a book-shop might find that he had difficulties because of the pornographic nature of some of the books on display. If he felt strongly enough about it he might discuss with his employer the possibility of not having to deal with those kind of books, which might lessen the problem for him. But no priest is going to ask him to leave his job just because he may be having problems with 'bad thoughts', unless he has another job to go to. On the other hand, some jobs involve an obvious and immediate occasion of sin, as in the case of a person whose work involved administering or providing the service in an abortion clinic. In such a situation it would not be possible to keep the job without participating repeatedly in something which is seriously wrong in itself.

There are particular difficulties for an unmarried couple living together, especially if they have children. If they are free to marry and have the intention of staying together, then marriage is the obvious course for them. But if one party is not free to marry because of a previous marriage, their continuing to live together makes it difficult for both of them to return to living according to the Gospel. On the other hand, if they have lived together for some years and become economically interdependent, and if they have children for whom they share a joint responsibility, they cannot easily separate. The challenge for a couple in this situation is to decide honestly how best they can be faithful to the requirements of the gospel, without neglecting the responsibilities in justice which they may have incurred as a result of their relationship. Whatever advice a priest may give them will be forward-looking and will aim at helping them to respond to this challenge.

As a general principle, if I want to avoid sin in the future, I have to try as far as possible to avoid the situations that lead to sin. The difficulty in doing that may in itself be a more than adequate penance for any of my past sins.

Prayer of sorrow

I wonder did you ever notice how some people are always saying 'sorry'; 'sorry, can I have the salt please?'; 'sorry' because I was standing in the doorway when you wanted to come in; 'sorry' because I asked you to do something for me. To a certain extent the word 'sorry' has become just a throw-away word in polite conversation, so that when we really want it to mean something it can sound a bit hollow and empty. But when it comes to celebrating forgiveness in the Sacrament of Reconciliation, sorrow for sin is one of the four main aspects of the celebration and it has a very definite meaning. It means that I repent of the fact that I have offended God and risked losing his love, and of the fact that I have offended others whom he loves.

The penitent is invited to express this sorrow in the form of an Act of Contrition (Act of Sorrow). All of us learned an Act of Contrition at school at some stage. The one I learned was:

> O my God, I am heartily sorry for all my sins, because they offend you, who are infinitely good, and I firmly resolve, with the help of your grace, never to offend you again.

Another one which I hear quite frequently in Confession nowadays goes:

> O my God, I thank you for loving me. I am sorry for all my sins, for not loving others and for not loving you. Help me to live like Jesus and not sin again. Amen.

But it may happen that you feel that you have grown out of the Act of Sorrow that you learnt at school, and that you wish to express your sorrow in a more personal way. This is entirely up to you. Some people who are inclined to get a bit nervous at Confession have difficulty in remembering the Act of Contrition even though they could say it perfectly ten minutes later. All that is necessary for the celebration of the Sacrament is that the penitent expresses his sorrow for sin and his intention of renewing his life with God's help. This can be done in a learnt prayer, in a passage of Scripture, or in his own words. For the benefit of those who might find them useful, a selection of these Prayers of Sorrow is included in an Appendix at the end of the book.

A young man came to talk to me some years ago and said he was worried because he had slept with his girlfriend. We talked for a while about the kind of relationship they had and why it wasn't appropriate for them to be sleeping together. He seemed to be happy enough to accept the Church's teaching as we had discussed it, and felt that intercourse should be kept for marriage. He thought that his girlfriend would probably agree, and that if they had thought more seriously about it beforehand, they might not have slept together at all. Throughout our conversation he seemed to be both mature and very honest. Up to this we hadn't talked about Confession, but I mentioned it then because

I felt it was appropriate. He said that he would like Confession, but he didn't think he could be forgiven because he couldn't honestly say that he was sorry. I was a bit surprised, but when I asked him what he meant, he said he still couldn't honestly say that he didn't enjoy sleeping with his girlfriend at the time.

Being sorry doesn't mean saying that the sin wasn't enjoyable or profitable at the time. Enjoyment, pleasure and profit are some of the main reasons why people sin in the first place, and there is nothing to be gained from denying the reality of the enjoyment. Sorrow is about recognising that what brought about the enjoyment, pleasure or profit was wrong. People are sometimes worried about saying that they are sorry because they know that they are weak and they might commit the same sin again in a few days. What is asked in the Sacrament of Reconciliation is that we have a sincere intention of avoiding sin in the future with God's help, not that we give a guarantee. With the best of intentions we are human, and we can't see into the future. Nobody understands that better than God.

On that understanding my visitor was happy to accept absolution. It's nice to meet someone who is so obviously sincere.

Absolution

The other important part of celebrating forgiveness is the forgiveness itself — the absolution. Up to the introduction of the new Rite of Penance in 1976 the absolution was given in Latin and was usually said by the priest at the same time as the penitent was saying the Act of Sorrow. In this way the good news of God's forgiveness was probably obscured for a lot of people. We knew that we were being forgiven, but we didn't really hear it at first hand. Even now, although the absolution is given in our own language after the Act of Sorrow, some of its richness may be lost because it's all over so quickly. The words of absolution are worth looking at a bit more closely.

The priest extends his hands over the penitent's head as a physical sign of forgiveness and says:

> God the Father of Mercies, through the death and Resurrection of his Son has reconciled the world to himself; he sent the Holy Spirit among us for the forgiveness of sins; through the ministry of the Church may God give you pardon and peace, and I absolve you from your sins in the name of the Father and of the Son and of the Holy Spirit.

In the Gospels we often hear of Jesus laying his hands on the blind, the deaf and the sick, and healing them. The hand is a symbol of power and authority. In many of the Sacraments the priest or bishop imposes hands on the person receiving the Sacrament as a symbol of the healing and strengthening power of God that comes to us through the ministry of the Church. The imposition of hands takes place in Baptism, Confirmation, Ordination and the Anointing of the Sick as well as in the Sacrament of Reconciliation.

The words of absolution themselves tell us a lot about the meaning of what we are celebrating. They tell us that it is God the Father's plan that we should all come to him and find eternal life and that for this reason Jesus his Son came among us. By his own life of perfect love and his willingness to die bearing witness to the truth of God's love, and by his rising to new life, Jesus reconciled us to the Father. He could reconcile us to the Father because, as one of us, Jesus' life was pleasing to God in a way that no human life had ever been. Because of the Father's great love and Jesus' love which is given to us in the Holy Spirit, God is patient with us and our sins can be forgiven.

The words of absolution also remind us that it is the will of Jesus that our sins should be forgiven, through the ministry of the Church. In other words, as we have seen before, our sin and our forgiveness is not a purely personal matter; it has a community dimension to it. We sin as members of a believing community, and we are forgiven as members of a believing community. Our reconciliation with God is also our reconciliation with the community. The priest prays that God will give me pardon *and* peace. This really is important. Some people go away from Confession forgiven but not at peace; still troubled by what they have confessed. Perhaps we don't trust God enough, or we think that like other people he will wait his chance and bring up our sins again at some stage in the future. It might just help to remember that when Jesus was arrested in the Garden of Gethsemane, all his disciples ran away and left him. At the foot of the cross the following day there was only Mary his Mother, John the youngest of the Apostles, and some of the other women. Yet after Easter his greeting to them all, on every occasion that is mentioned in the Gospel is 'Peace be with you'. He not only forgave them for their betrayal but offered them his peace. That's what he offers us in the Sacrament of

Reconciliation — forgiveness *and* peace. We may still have to cope with some of the practical difficulties caused by our sin, but we can do so in the knowledge that we are at peace and at one with God once we have confessed sincerely and received his absolution.

Finally, we are forgiven 'in the name of the Father and of the Son and of the Holy Spirit'. It isn't just human forgiveness we receive, it is the forgiveness of the God who created us, who came to show us his love, and who is with us still as we try our best to follow his call. Sometimes, when I am hearing Confessions, I get a bit tired or I'm not on the top of my form. There are times when I feel that *I* haven't helped the person very much in human terms. But I believe that it is God who really gives the help and the forgiveness and the peace, and so at a time like that I often pray that he will make up to the person for my human limitations, so that nothing will come between that person and the gift of God's forgiveness and peace. I'm sure other priests often feel the same.

In the box
People have different preferences when it comes to going to Confession. Some people feel more comfortable in the dark and others prefer a bit of light; some like to sit while others prefer to kneel. The possibility of remaining anonymous is very important to some and not so important to others, who may actually prefer to go to a priest who knows them. There should really be as much flexibility about this as possible. For instance, if it bothers you to have the light on there's no reason why you shouldn't ask the priest to turn it down or off, and likewise if you would prefer a bit of light there's no harm in saying so.

Confessionals vary a lot from church to church. Some of them are reasonably comfortable without being luxurious, but others are fairly grim. Whatever way the Confessional is designed, it should be appropriate to the *celebration* of a Sacrament, while at the same time guaranteeing the privacy of the penitent. It shouldn't be a place which is going to make the penitent feel uncomfortable, or in which the priest and penitent risk contracting pneumonia.

A lot of newer churches now have confessionals which offer the penitent the alternative of confessing in a kneeling position behind the traditional screen, or sitting in a chair facing the priest.

With a little bit of imagination this kind of confessional could be provided in most churches. The best-designed confessionals which I have seen, offering reasonable comfort, privacy and an atmosphere of celebration, were each constructed some time after the church in which they are situated.

It seems to me that the preference for the face-to-face approach and for the more anonymous form of celebration is about equal. Ideally, every church should be able to provide both. Perhaps this is something which could be considered by priests and parishioners together, and which, with mutual co-operation, could be achieved without too much expense or difficulty.

The communal celebration of Reconciliation

Many parishes now have communal celebrations of Reconciliation at Christmas and Easter. Everyone wishing to participate gathers in the church and the celebration begins with an appropriate hymn or piece of music. Then the people have the opportunity of listening to one or more passages of scripture on the theme of reconciliation, followed by a few words from the celebrant. The celebrant or one of the assistants leads the people in an examination of conscience and a prayer of sorrow. At this point in the celebration, a number of priests take up their positions at various points in the church, and each person present is invited to make a simple individual Confession to the priest of his choice, and to receive absolution. During the Confessions the choir or folk group might provide some appropriate music. The celebration concludes with a prayer of thanksgiving and a final blessing.

The big advantage of these celebrations, of course, is the fact that they help to emphasise the community dimension of sin and forgiveness. When I see the people up the road and the people around the corner confessing their sins, it can be an encouragement for me to seek forgiveness too. There is often a very real sense of a community praying for each other. It is easier in a community celebration to be conscious of one's responsibilities as a member of the community, and one's need to be reconciled to be community.

It was a disadvantage, when these celebrations first began to take place, that people sometimes used to refer to them as the 'easy confession' or the 'quick confession'. Many people seemed to get the impression that the actual confession of sins was not necessary in these communal celebrations of reconciliation. What is expected of each of us in the Sacrament of Reconciliation is the same whether it is celebrated privately in the confessional or at a communal celebration. Each penitent is expected to confess any grave sin of which he may be aware after an examination of conscience, which has not already been forgiven in a previous confession. No person is expected to agonise over things which have been forgotten and, if there is something which a person genuinely cannot bring himself to mention at the time, he is not required to confess it then in order to receive absolution.

For a person who might be nervous or anxious about confession, or who has not been to confession for a long time, the advantage of a communal celebration is not that it is a 'quickie' or that he doesn't have to confess anything. It is the sense of solidarity with the rest of the community, and the knowledge that whatever he confesses there will be no need for details and no questions asked. For the same reason, it follows that a person who wishes to discuss some detail of her confession or to ask for guidance from the priest, would not find the communal celebration the best occasion for doing so. Ideally, a regularly practising Catholic should consider joining in the communal celebration once or twice each year, and also making a 'private' confession from time to time during the year. The two types of celebration are intended more to complement each other than to be alternatives.

Children and Confession

A child's early experiences are particularly important in helping to form positive attitudes. This is no less true where the Sacrament of Reconciliation is concerned. Parents and other adults should take care to speak about the Sacrament in a positive way and, as far as possible, not to pass on to children any anxieties or fears which they themselves may have about it. Feelings of shame, anxiety or punishment should not be associated with Confession. Priests, like policemen, and the mythical 'bogey man' are sometimes held as a threat by frustrated parents over young children. It is easy to sympathise with parents who are sometimes under a lot of pressure, but to say to a child, 'Behave yourself, the priest is looking at you', or 'if you don't stop that, I'll give you to the priest', doesn't do much for a child's confidence in priests or in the Sacraments.

Priests often say how sad it is that many young children go very rarely to Communion or Confession once they have celebrated these Sacraments for the first time. This is sometimes due to the fact that their parents don't go. With Confession, just as with Communion, it is far better for parents to come with their children then to send them alone. Sometimes young children are nervous of the confessional, though what they are taught at school should help them to see Confession as a joyful celebration, a coming back to Jesus.

It would be a very helpful thing if parents would become familiar with the way Confession is dealt with in the primary school religion programme, and especially with the prayers which they are taught for use at Confession, which are specially suited to their age. Most teachers will be only too happy to help parents to do this.

In the final analysis, children will learn more about the meaning of forgiveness, and the need to forgive, through their own experience of patience, tolerance and forgiveness at home. For most young children, parents are somewhere in the same general category as God, and what they see in their parents is what they will expect from God. Even in their own work and play, they can experience the sense of loss and hurt after a disagreement. If they can be encouraged to seek reconciliation at that level, they will have no fear of asking God too for his forgiveness.

Summary
1. Confession is about honesty, not about telling God something he hasn't heard before.
2. Penance is an aid to renewal, not a punishment for sin.
3. Sorrow is a recognition that something was wrong; not a statement that I never meant it or didn't enjoy it.
4. Forgiveness means that what divided us before no longer does so, and it will not be held against me in the future.
5. A good celebration is helped by a suitable environment.

For reflection

1. What is my image of penance?
2. How is the Sacrament of Reconciliation celebrated in my parish? What if anything could I/we do to improve it?
3. What experience of forgiveness do my children have? What image of God and his forgiveness do I convey to them?

7

THE QUESTIONS PEOPLE ASK

The Sacrament of Reconciliation is primarily a celebration of forgiveness and a personal encounter with the God who forgives. But it is also, in human terms, the beginning of a new stage in the process of healing and growth. People sometimes find that, although the desire to renew their lives is there, they need a fuller understanding of the Church's teaching or a broader vision of some question in order to be able to see the way ahead more clearly. John *wants* to restore the relationship with his sister which has been soured for years because of an argument over their father's will. But how does he go about it? He can't shake off the feelings of bitterness. Mary *wants* to get back to regular participation in the Mass, but somehow the joy of celebration just isn't there anymore.

When celebrating the Sacrament of Reconciliation, people frequently express their doubts or anxieties about the future, or seek guidance in charting the way forward. This chapter will examine some of the areas in which people seem to find difficulty, and make some tentative proposals as to how these difficulties might be approached in a positive way. In the course of doing so, we will be tying up some loose ends which have been left in the previous chapters.

Why should I go to Mass when I don't get anything out of it?
The first thing to take account of, I suppose, is that the Mass is a community prayer. This means that it will be a bit more difficult to be fully involved in it at times when I am not particularly switched on to the community, and at times when I am not particularly switched on to prayer. So, to begin with, there will be times for all of us when we are not in the best form for celebrating Mass. As a priest this is still true. I say Mass a few mornings a week at 8.00 a.m. and it's sometimes hard to be fully awake. Another day I have Mass at lunch-time and sometimes it can be difficult, in the middle of a busy day, just

to slow the pace down and be a bit prayerful. At the off-times, all any of us can do is put our best into it. As far as Sunday Mass is concerned, if you find it's not going too well, maybe one thing you could consider is what time is most suited to your lifestyle; when are you likely to be at your best for Mass — Saturday evening, Sunday morning (earlier or later), or Sunday evening?

Another thing to ask yourself is why you are there anyway. Are you there because you've always been there, or because you feel you have to, or because you really want to? I'm not suggesting that people should stop going to Mass except when they want to, but I do think that we often resist doing things that other people think we should do. People sometimes say 'I'm only a Catholic because I was born a Catholic'. As far as I'm concerned, I started off as a Catholic because of the family I was born into, but I'd like to think that the reason I am still one is because I have come to know Jesus Christ, and to understand to some extent his love for me. Maybe it will help if you can make it your own personal choice to be there.

Of course, no matter where you go to, if you make up your mind beforehand that it is going to be boring, then it will be — nothing surer. People who expect to be bored at Mass often arrive late and just sit and wait for it to end. But who ever heard of going to a party to watch? It may sound like a cliché, but the best way to get something out is to put something in; participation is what it's all about. If you've been switched off for a while, it might be difficult to get back into a positive frame of mind all of a sudden. How about trying it a bit at a time? Each Sunday try to be there a few minutes before Mass begins, and find a place from where you can see what's going on. Before Mass starts, choose some particular part of it that you are going to concentrate on especially this week; it might be the Gospel, the Consecration, the Offertory, the Communion. Without ignoring the rest of the liturgy, put everything you have into the part you have chosen. As the weeks go by, you should find that the liturgy means more to you because you are entering into it more. Sometimes people don't feel part of the community at Mass and they're so cautious at the sign of peace you would think they were shaking hands with a rattlesnake. It might be an idea just to try and be a bit more aware of the other people around you at Mass. After a while you will begin to recognise them, and then celebrating with them will make a bit more sense.

Many ordinary human factors can also affect our feelings about prayer and Mass over a period of time. If I am not in the best of health or if I am anxious or over-worked, these things can make it more difficult for me to give my attention to the Mass and then I feel as if it is wasted. Feelings are important, but the Mass is never a waste just because it didn't feel good. My inability to concentrate doesn't stop God from giving his gifts.

It may be worth mentioning too, that people sometimes find that going to Mass and praying on their own just doesn't work out for them if there is some other aspect of their life which is seriously out of line with the Gospel. I may not make the connection at the time, but if my relationship with God is damaged seriously by sin, and I have any kind of a conscience, then I am scarcely going to feel particularly at ease in his presence until I have first been reconciled with him and have started to put right whatever was wrong. It was Jesus himself who said:

> So then, if you are bringing your offering to the altar and there remember that your brother has something against you, leave your offering there before the altar, go and be reconciled with your brother first, and then come back and present your offering.
>
> *(Matthew 5:23)*

How could I constantly cheat my customers, or carry a bitter grudge, or have an ongoing affair behind my wife's back, and then expect Mass to feel the same as it always did?

Why won't they listen to me?

I know the 'generation gap' is really meant to be a phenomenon of the 1960s but I think it will always be with us. Actually, the generation gap is not a problem, it's how we handle it that causes the problem. People are formed and influenced to a large extent by their own experience of the world around them and, just as the experience of two individuals will be different, so the experience of two generations will be different, expecially so in this century which has seen such rapid and radical development and change.

The problem arises when we allow our different experiences to come between us; when we write one another off as old fogies and young fools; and especially when we assume that everything that is traditional is out of date, or that everything new is seditious and immoral. From one generation to the next there are always some truths and values that are worth holding on to, and there's nothing wrong with being conservative if 'conservative' means protecting what is of lasting value. It could reasonably be argued that humanity has only survived this long because there have always been some people with adaptability and drive *and* other people with caution and a sense of tradition.

Where the generation gap sometimes causes problems is when young people reach the stage of having many interests and commitments outside the home. It may seem to parents that they no longer have an interest in the family and that they have no sense of responsibility. It may seem to the younger generation that the parents don't understand the importance of all the things they are involved in, and that they have forgotten what it is like to be young (if they were ever young). When children are young, their world is largely enclosed in the world of their family. As they grow older and into adulthood their world expands, sometimes faster than they can handle. Understanding is not as automatic as it was before because now the life experience is not the same. John is up in Dublin working on computers; Pauline is flying off to a new job in Australia next month; Margaret is moving out of the city to marry a farmer from Kildare. If there is a solution to the problems caused by the generation gap it lies in making time to be together, time to talk *and* to listen. What is called for is generosity with one's time and oneself.

How far can I go with my boyfriend/girlfriend?

I think this question is part of a broader question; 'How far can I go with people?' *or* 'How should I express my relationships with other people?' If I meet a casual aquaintance in the street, I may stop and say hello and perhaps shake hands but, unless I am very insincere, I won't behave towards him in the same way that I behave towards a long-time friend. On the one hand, it would seem out of place to embrace the postman when he arrives in the morning or to give the lady at the Revenue Commissioners a little peck on the cheek; on the other hand, a couple who have been going out together for two years are scarcely going to limit themselves to shaking hands at the end of an evening out. It's really all a question of honesty or truth.

Does this particular way of acting really reflect the true nature of our relationship? If someone asks me 'How far can I go...?', it seems to me that she is saying 'I feel that my relationship with my boyfriend is growing stronger, and I want to express our closeness in a physical way, but I'm not sure at just what point it might become sinful'. Obviously people who are interested in 'one night stands' or short-term relationships don't ask this kind of question because they are not really interested in depth or commitment of any kind.

So, let's begin with the bottom line; sexual intercourse is the expression of total commitment and so it is only honest or appropriate where a couple have made that kind of commitment, i.e. in marriage. The thing a lot of people overlook is the fact that, at the more intimate level, different degrees of physical contact or activity are not just separate events, unrelated to each other, but rather part of a process leading towards intercourse. Once the process begins it can be difficult to stop, and can create frustration and disillusionment. I often think the experience could be compared to togging-out and getting warmed up for a game of football and then finding that the game is off because the referee hasn't arrived.

Nobody sets out to hurt the one he loves. If you killed your girlfriend in a car accident you would be heartbroken, so you take care and you don't take unnecessary risks and you don't show off. In the same way, if we accept that intercourse is not yet appropriate to our relationship, we avoid the kind of activity that is most closely related to it so as not to take the risk of hurting or being dishonest with one another. In the cold light of day it is easy to feel that we are in full control, but in the heat of the moment it doesn't always work out that way. For this reason I believe that unmarried couples sleeping together, however good their intentions, place too great a strain on their self-control.

To go back to the image of the car; I wonder how many accidents happen because of people wanting to show off and to prove themselves? It is sad that in relationships young people often feel that they have to prove themselves. So the young man may feel that if he doesn't get fairly physical with his girlfriend after the first few night out, she will think he's not that much of a man. The young woman equally may feel under pressure to allow her boyfriend to take things further than she really wants, because she doesn't want to appear unresponsive in case she is dropped. My experience in the confessional would suggest that many couples fall into the trap of imagining one another's expectations and then trying to live up to them. Obviously, if the relationship appears to be growing deeper, it makes sense for a couple to discuss their hopes, fears and expectations and to have some kind of idea of where they are going and what their limits are. The old idea that 'if you love me enough you will respect my beliefs and be prepared to wait till the time is right', is still a good test for a mature Christian relationship.

Having said all that, it must be recognised that couples who are genuinely in love will not always find it easy to get the balance just right. If they share a common understanding of their relationship, they can help one another, so that when one is weak the other is strong. If they can agree on the various things which help them or which make things difficult for them it can contribute to getting things right. It is certainly not in the spirit of the Gospel that they should think of their sexual feelings as wrong, or be afraid of their sexuality, but only that they should have respect for its full significance. St Augustine is reputed to have prayed, 'Lord make me pure — but not yet'. His problem is not unusual. A lot of us would like to do what is right, except that we'd also like to do what is not right. It is the practical and mature decisions we make that help to get things in balance; to make no decision and just leave things to chance is really to have made the wrong decision. In the end, of course, if we do fail, God is forgiving and calls us always to a fresh beginning.

Why don't I seem to be able to pray?

Thousands of books have been written on the topic of prayer, and all kinds of methods of praying have been suggested down through the centuries, so there's not a lot that I can add. At the same time, difficulties with prayer are often mentioned by people in Confession and it may be worth making a few suggestions here.

'Father, I get terrible distractions. I can't keep my mind on my prayers'. I think there are really two kinds of distractions, the ones outside me (mechanical diggers, wasps, someone laughing or talking in the next room) and the ones within myself (my excitement, anxiety, tiredness, pain etc.). The best way to deal with the outside distractions is to pay attention to them for a few minutes. Listen consciously to the mechanical digger and then after a little while just let it fade into the background. When we try to shut out distractions we only become more conscious of them. For the distractions that come from within, sometimes the best approach is to talk to God about them first and then get on with whatever prayer I want. 'Lord, I'm sitting here in this church because I want to spend a bit of time with you, but it's freezing cold and I'm not in the best of form, because my work went against me today and I'm worried that this job I'm on is coming unstuck', and so on. To put it simply, don't hide from distractions, bring them in and get them on your side.

Probably the biggest difficulty most of us have about praying is getting around to it. We find it hard to make the time, so when we do pray we expect to be able to switch on immediately. But it's like starting a car from cold, we need a bit of time to warm up. To begin with, it helps to pick a time when I don't have a sense of being too rushed. Then it is good to spend a little time just relaxing, reminding myself that God is present with me, wherever I happen to be. Many of the well-known writers on prayer suggest that a lot has to do with being both alert and relaxed at the same time. It's amazing how, just by sitting in a comfortable but erect position and breathing gently in and out in a regular pattern, it is possible to become quite relaxed and ready for prayer after about five minutes. Too often we dive into it without giving ourselves the opportunity of relaxing.

One other thing about prayer, which I think people are beginning to become more conscious of, is that prayer doesn't have to be all talk. Like any relationship, my relationship with God involves both talking to him and listening to him, and some of the time just being with him.

Sometimes my talking to him dries up because I just don't have anything particular to say at the time. Of course, my talking to God can be a bit selfish sometimes, if I spend all my time talking about myself. It is good to pray about my hopes and anxieties about the needs and situations of others, and of the world in general, and to express my trust in him, that he is concerned about these as well. He is, after all, not just my God.

It is good to listen to what God has to say to us about ourselves and about himself. I don't mean that we should be listening for voices in the night, but we do find his word in Scripture, and to spend a few minutes reading and reflecting on a passage from the Gospel is just as much a prayer as anything we say to God. In the same way, a crucifix or religious object, or any of the beautiful things of nature, can speak to us in their own way of God's goodness and love.

If you have ever gone walking with a good friend, you may have noticed how it is possible to walk for ages without saying anything. This is not the same as the silence which we experience when people are uncomfortable or embarrassed or shy; it is the silence of being completely at ease with each other. Being with God in quietness is prayer too and if, as time goes on, you want to say something there's nothing to prevent it.

Is it all right to go to Communion regularly without Confession?

It is a very special wish of Jesus that we should receive Communion as a way of uniting ourselves with him and with each other. Only one thing can prevent us from doing so, and that is if our relationship with God is destroyed by serious sin. It makes sense that it would be hypocritical to gather around the altar and receive communion if, in my heart, I am separated from God and from his people. If I have sinned seriously, it is only natural that I should first ask forgiveness through the Sacrament of Reconciliation, and then celebrate my unity with God and the community. Who would arrive into a friend's house after a serious disagreement, and sit down at the table, without first being reconciled with his friend?

If I have sinned in a less serious way, then my friendship with God is affected but not destroyed, and my links with the community are strained but not broken. More than ever in this situation, I need to receive Christ in the Eucharist, in order to renew my relationship with him and with the community.

What can I do about bad thoughts?

Thoughts of hatred, jealousy, and ingratitude as well as many others would come under the heading of 'bad thoughts'. In practice, however, most people use the term to refer to inappropriate sexual thoughts. 'Bad thoughts' are a bit like distractions in prayer. The more you try to push them away, the more conscious of them you become. So the first thing I would suggest about bad thoughts is to ignore them in so far as it is possible. It is not always possible to control one's imagination. If there is a serious problem with bad thoughts, it might be worth considering whether there is anything in particular which is giving rise to them, e.g. reading inappropriate books, participating by choice in inappropriate conversations. A good way to get beyond 'bad thoughts' in relation to any particular person is to concentrate on getting to know the person as a person, complete with family, friends, interests, fears and hopes. In this way the body is noticed as part of the whole person, and not in isolation.

I think it is worth making a distinction between 'lust' and 'sexual awareness'. Peter is twenty-two and works in a large office. Some of the girls in the office are very good-looking and attractive. Peter is not blind and he is conscious of their sexuality, their dress, their ways of moving, their ways of speaking and reacting, and the fact that they are different, not just physically but in other ways as well. In other words, Peter is a fairly normal person, who is sexually aware, and has sexual feelings, and notices what is going on around him. Not everything he notices would be appropriate material for a conversation with his male colleagues.

Michael works in the same office, but his reaction to his female colleagues is different. He enjoys embarrassing them with smart comments. He spends a lot of time mentally undressing them and imagining what they would be like in bed. He shares his imagination with his male colleagues over their tea break. That is what is meant by looking at a woman lustfully, and that is where the sin comes in, because it reduces a woman from being a person to being an object of sexual gratification for someone else. Naturally the difference between awareness and lust can work the other way too. A woman can, through her wrong attitude, reduce men to the level of objects of her sexual desire.

Why can't I forgive?

A young man I know was badly let down, time and time again, by his brother, who was also his partner in business. The brother kept taking money out of the business and using it in wasteful ways on projects of his own. The trust between them was completely broken down, and the business eventually collapsed, leaving the young man to support a wife and two young children on what little they could salvage from the remains of the company. He lost his house and they had to move into smaller rented accommodation. 'How can God seriously expect me to forgive my brother after all he did, not just once but many times? I'm going around with this lump inside my chest and every time

I see him I boil over.' When Peter asked Jesus, 'How often must I forgive my brother?' Jesus said 'I tell you, not seven times, but seventy times seven times'. Now that's a tall order, and still Jesus makes it a condition for his willingness for forgive us. We will not be forgiven unless we forgive 'our brother' from our hearts.

The first step towards recovery in any situation is always the recognition that it has happened. When someone we trust betrays that trust, it hurts a lot. It is important to face the reality; the company is gone, and the house is gone, and no end of bitterness will change that. In fact bitterness only takes up the energy we need to rebuild. Revenge and bearing grudges is totally destructive for ourselves, not to mention anyone else.

One thing that makes forgiveness more difficult is that we sometimes confuse forgiving with forgetting. Jesus doesn't ask us to forget, which in many cases would be impossible. What he asks us is not to allow the memory we have of the past to sour the future. That is not to say that forgiveness is easy; no, it takes a lot of courage, just as it takes courage to accept forgiveness too. But the important point is that there is no question of pretending that nothing ever happened and that we can all be just the same to each other as we were before. To extend forgiveness is to recognise that something happened which shouldn't have happened. It is to say that I am willing to take steps to rebuild over the time ahead the friendship, the trust and the love that was there before, and in the future I will not use the past against you. It doesn't mean that I should immediately restore you to the same position of trust, which might only put too great a pressure on the new relationship.

Strange as it may seem, it is possible to forgive, even when the other person is not yet ready to receive forgiveness. The one thing that really destroys any hope of reconciliation is the attitude of each person waiting for the other to make the first move. Too many old friends have died enemies, because neither would take the risk of making the first move. Frank O'Connor paints a vivid picture of stubbornness in his story, 'The Luceys'.

> 'And you're going to make the same mistake with your brother that you made with your son?'
>
> 'I'm not forgetting that either, Charliss,' said Tom. 'It wasn't today nor yesterday that I thought of it'.

And it isn't as if you didn't care for him', Charlie went on remorselessly. 'It isn't as if you had no heart for him. You know he's lying up there waiting for you. He sent for you last night and you never came. He had the bottle of whiskey and the two glasses by the bed. All he wants is for you to say you forgive him... Jesus Christ, man,' he shouted with all the violence in him aroused, 'never mind what you're doing to him. Do you know what you're doing to yourself?'

A last word

This book began with the idea of God's forgiveness. Jesus himself presented us with the image of the Father who searches for his lost sheep until he has found it, and then carries it home rejoicing. It is, perhaps, appropriate that we end with the question of our forgiveness of each other. It is our calling as Christians, not just to be forgiven, but to be people who forgive, and who bring God's healing to each other.

I hope that this book will help those who read it to discover an inner peace and a new sense of celebration in the Sacrament of Reconciliation and that, through this, our sense of community and our mutual understanding may be enhanced.

8

A MODEL FOR
INDIVIDUAL CONFESSION

The following outline is given for the benefit of anyone who may find it helpful to have a definite structure for celebrating the Sacrament of Reconciliation. Of all the Sacraments it is probably the most personal, and nobody should feel anxious about saying things exactly as they were learnt at school, ten or even forty years ago. It is what we have to say, and what our attitude is that concerns God, not the use of exact formulas.

At some time before the Confession, the penitent should spend some time in an examination of conscience. If she hasn't been for some time, or hasn't been regularly to Confession, then there may be a need for a slightly more detailed examination of conscience than otherwise.

When the penitent enters the confessional the celebration of the Sacrament takes place roughly as follows:

1. *The priest welcomes the penitent warmly and puts her at her ease.*

2. *Priest and penitent together:*
    'In the name of the Father and of the Son and of the Holy Spirit. Amen.'

3. *The priest invites the penitent to make her confession, trusting in God's love and readiness to forgive. He may use some words from Scripture.*

4. *Penitent:*
    Father, it is . . . . . . weeks since my last Confession. I am a married woman with two young children. I have just recently gone back to work now that the youngest is six months old.
    (*This kind of background information helps the priest to understand better anything the penitent may say later on.*)

5. *The priest may read a short passage from Scripture, which serves as an invitation to conversion and renewal. This is part of the new Rite, but it hasn't, unfortunately, become common practice.*

6. *Penitent:*
    Since my last Confession I have sinned in a number of ways for which I want to ask God's forgiveness. I did .... I failed to do ...... and it led to .... One thing I have noticed over the past while is that I have developed a bad attitude towards ...... which is at the root of a number of my sins. I am happy that, since my last Confession I have seen an improvement in relation to .... In general I would say that my life as a Christian is ....

7. *The priest may make some comment or ask some question about what the penitent has confessed, not to make her embarrassed, but in case there is a need for any clarification or help on his part. Then he proposes some form of penance to her or discusses with her what might be appropriate. Then:*

    Is there anything else worrying you?
    At this point the penitent may wish to ask the priest for advice on some particular matter. Bearing in mind the possibility that others may be waiting, the priest may suggest arranging to see the penitent if it appears that more time is needed than the situation allows.

8. *The penitent expresses her sorrow, either in her own words or in a formal prayer of sorrow (c.f.* **Chapter 9 — A selection of acts of sorrow**).

9. *Priest:*
    God the Father of mercies, through the death and resurrection of His Son, has reconciled the world to himself and sent the Holy Spirit among us for the forgiveness of sins; through the ministry of the Church may God give you pardon and peace, and I absolve you from your sins in the name of the Father and of the Son and of the Holy Spirit.

10. *Penitent:*
    Amen.

11. *Priest:*
    The priest may give praise to God in a brief prayer or snippet of
    Scripture, concluding with the words:
    'Go in peace, your sins are forgiven'.

12. *Penitent:*
    Thanks be to God.

*When the celebration of the Sacrament is over, the penitent leaves the
Confessional, and should spend a little time in thanksgiving to God. The
penance should be completed as soon as possible. If at any stage during
the Confession, the penitent is unsure of what to do or has any difficulty,
then she should just say so to the priest who will be able to help.*

9

A SELECTION
OF ACTS OF SORROW

The following selection of Acts of Sorrow is taken from the **Rite of Penance.** Some of them are based on Scripture, others are traditional in style, and still others are more modern in their expression. A penitent is, of course, free to use any other appropriate Act of Sorrow, or to use his own words.

1. Remember, Lord, your compassion and mercy you showed long ago.
    Do not recall the sins and failings of my youth.
    In your mercy remember me Lord, because of your goodness.

2. Wash me from my guilt and cleanse me from my sin.
    I acknowledge my offence; my sin is before me always.

3. Father, I have sinned against you and am not worthy to be called your Son. Be merciful to me a sinner.

4. Father of mercy, like the prodigal son I return to you and say: 'I have sinned against you and am no longer worthy to be called your son.' Christ Jesus, Saviour of the World, I pray with the repentant thief to whom you promised paradise: 'Lord, remember me in your kingdom.' Holy Spirit, fountain of love, I call on you with trust: 'Purify my heart, and help me to walk as a child of the light.'

5. Lord Jesus, you opened the eyes of the blind, healed the sick, forgave the sinful woman and, after Peter's denial, confirmed him in your love. Listen to my prayer; forgive all my sins, renew your love in my heart, help me to live in perfect unity with my fellow Christians that I may proclaim your saving power to all the world.

6. Lord Jesus, you choose to be called the friend of sinners. By your saving death and resurrection free me from my

sins. May your peace take root in my heart and bring forth a harvest of love, holiness, and truth.

7. Lord Jesus Christ, you are the Lamb of God; you take away the sins of the world. Through the grace of the Holy Spirit restore me to friendship with your Father, cleanse me from every stain of sin in the blood you shed for me, and raise me to new life for the glory of your name.

8. Lord God, in your goodness have mercy on me; do not look on my sins but take away all my guilt. Create in me a clean heart and renew within me an upright spirit.

9. Lord Jesus, Son of God, have mercy on me a sinner.

10. My God, I am sorry for my sins with all my heart. In choosing to do wrong and failing to do good, I have sinned against you whom I should love above all things. I firmly intend with your help, to do penance, to sin no more, and to avoid whatever leads me to sin. Our Saviour Jesus Christ suffered and died for us. In his name, have mercy.

11. O my God, because you are good, I am very sorry that I have sinned against you, and with the help of your grace I will not sin again.

12. O my God, I am sorry and beg pardon for all my sins, and detest them above all things, because they deserve your dreadful punishments, because they have crucified my loving saviour Jesus Christ, and most of all, because they offend your infinite goodness; and I firmly resolve, by the help of your grace, never to offend you again, and carefully to avoid the occasions of sin.

13. O my God, I am heartily sorry for all my sins, because they offend you, who are infinitely good, and I firmly resolve, with the help of your grace, never to offend you again.

14. God our Father, I thank you for loving me. I am sorry for all my sins, for what I have done and for what I have failed to do. I will sincerely try to love you and others in everything I do and say. Help me to walk in your light today and always.